D0535711

The Story Travelers Bible

created by **Tracey Madder**

illustrated by **Tim Crecelius**

Tyndale House Publishers, Inc.
Carol Stream, Illinois

Visit Tyndale's website for kids at www.tyndale.com/kids.

Visit Tracey Madder online at www.traceymadder.com.

The Story Travelers Bible

Designed by Jacqueline L. Nuñez

Edited by Sarah Rubio

For manufacturing information regarding this product, please call 1-800-323-9400.

For information about special discounts for bulk purchases, please contact Tyndale House Publishers at csresponse@tyndale.com or call 800-323-9400.

Library of Congress Cataloging-in-Publication Data

Names: Madder, Tracey, author. | Crecelius, Tim, illustrator.
Title: The story travelers Bible / created by Tracey Madder ; illustrated by Tim Crecelius.
Description: Carol Stream, Illinois : Tyndale House Publishers, [2017] | Audience: Ages 4-8.
Identifiers: LCCN 2016029011 | ISBN 9781496409157 (hc)
Subjects: LCSH: Bible—Antiquities—Juvenile literature. | Bible—History of contemporary events—Juvenile literature. | Bible—Study and teaching. | Bible stories, English.
Classification: LCC BS621 .M2735 2017 | DDC 220.95/05—dc23 LC record available at https://lccn.loc.gov/2016029011

Printed in China

23 22 21 20 19 18 17
7 6 5 4 3 2 1

To my parents with love—Thank you for instilling in me the belief that all things are possible. With God, they are!

T. M.

To my loving parents, Scott and Mary, whose encouragement and faith made me who I am.

T. C.

Contents

Acknowledgments

A special thank you to the entire team at Tyndale, Tim Crecelius for your extraordinary gifts, Dan Pierson for your encouragement, and my family for your love and support. I'd also like to thank Sarah Rubio, the best editor in the world, who not only inspires me to write better but also is a true example of a Christian woman, mother, and friend.

Introduction

Lana and Griffin walk down a church hallway, heading toward the pastor's office. Lana pauses to admire a brightly colored sign that reads "Vacation Bible School—Getting to Know God."

"Come on." Griffin says. "We only have 13 minutes and 58 seconds of lunch break left."

"Just a second." Lana catches Griffin's sleeve as he passes her. "This is the one I painted. What do you think of the colors?"

"They're great," Griffin says, barely glancing at the poster. "But we still need to find Munch. I hope Pastor Rick is finished lecturing him."

"Well, he shouldn't have been playing with his motorized extendable back scratcher during class," Lana says.

"I did have an itch on my back," Griffin explains. "It's one of his better inventions, if you ask me."

Vacation
Getting to

Lana just shakes her head. “Griffin,” she says after a moment, “what do you think Mrs. Morgan meant when she said that the best way to get to know God is to read his Word? Do you think she meant the WHOLE Bible?”

“I guess. What else would she mean?”

“It’s just—” Lana looks around to make sure no one is listening. “There are some parts of the Bible, well”—her voice drops to a whisper—“I skip over.”

Griffin doesn’t say anything.

“I read some of the Bible,” Lana says quickly. “I love a lot of the stories, and some of the letters are nice. But some of the stories just feel so strange to me. I can’t picture the people or places at all. Sometimes they don’t seem, well . . . real.”

“I don’t really read the Bible at all,” Griffin admits. “I just like the maps.”

“I guess neither of us really knows God then,” Lana says.

"Guess not," Griffin replies. An uncomfortable silence falls. "Let's just find Munch so we can eat," Griffin says finally.

When they reach Pastor Rick's office, neither the pastor nor Munch is anywhere to be found. Griffin finally spots their friend through the office window. Munch is outside on the lawn, tinkering with a rusted old minibus. Lana and Griffin leave the church building to meet up with him.

"Where's Pastor Rick?" Lana asks, approaching Munch.

"I don't know. He listened to what happened, then told me I could come out here and look at this hunk of junk," Munch says. He kicks the flat tire of the minibus and a few parts fall to the ground. Leaning over the engine, he tightens a bolt.

"You didn't get in trouble?" Griffin asks.

"Nope."

The engine of the minibus sputters. Startled, Munch jumps back. The engine coughs and smokes, shaking the whole vehicle. With each shake, the minibus changes. As the kids watch, the tires inflate, rust is replaced with gleaming red paint, and the cracked windows are suddenly whole and sparkling.

"Spinning sprockets," Munch whispers, dropping his wrench. Lana and Griffin just stare.

Three musical notes chime from the minibus. "Please climb aboard," a pleasant voice says. Munch heads for the bus door.

"Munch!" Lana squeaks. Ignoring her, Munch disappears inside. Seconds later, he pops his head out the window. "Look what I found," he says, dangling a map between two fingers.

"You've got my attention," Griffin says, darting toward the bus door.

"Lana, you coming?" Munch asks. Lana approaches the minibus with caution. She slowly climbs the stairs and looks around at the shabby interior. "Most of the seats have holes in them," she says. The minibus shakes once more, and suddenly the seats are gleaming as if brand new. Looking a bit pale, Lana chooses the seat directly across from the two boys and sits down. She notices a large Bible lying on the seat next to her.

The engine comes to life with a healthy roar. The minibus spins, as if caught in a whirlwind. Then it vanishes into thin air, taking the three children with it.

The Journey Begins

It is dark.

Very dark.

The darkness is so vast and empty that Lana, Munch, and Griffin can't even speak. They just sit in the deep, still, quiet darkness.

Then they hear a voice.

"Let there be light." A voice like that—a voice so powerful it can create anything out of nothing—could only be God's. The light glows against the black emptiness as God separates it from the darkness. "Day!" laughs God, making the light dance. He gestures to the darkness. "Night," he whispers.

On the second day, God forms the sky. "The sky will separate the waters above from the waters below," God says. He admires how the light ripples across the water.

God creates land on the third day, and plants of all kinds spring from the earth. The fragrance of roses, hibiscus, and lilacs fills the air. God takes a deep breath. "This is good," he says.

On the fourth day, God once again turns his gaze toward the sky. "Let lights appear to mark seasons, days, and years," he says. God makes the sun and moon. "I will place them in the sky to shine on the earth," he says. God also makes the stars—so many that only he can count them. "This is good," he says.

On the fifth day, God makes birds of all colors. Streaks of red, blue, and yellow dart through the air. "Let the waters be filled with fish and other life," God says. So he makes aquatic creatures of all shapes and sizes. Looking around, he says, "This is good." He blesses his new animals, telling them, "Be fruitful. Multiply—fill the sky and the seas!"

On the sixth day, God makes land animals. They run, fly, climb, and crawl through the beautiful Garden that God has created. God loves everything that he has made. But he's not finished yet.

God speaks once more.

"Let's make man," God says. He makes a man and then a woman. "The man and the woman are made in my image. They are the best thing I have created," God says. "They will rule over the fish and the birds and the animals. I give them my world to care for."

On the seventh day, God rests.

To learn more about Creation, read Genesis 1.

God looked over all he had made, and he saw that it was very good!

Genesis 1:31

Fellow Travelers

"Spinning sprockets!" Munch says. "Where did the bus take us?" He stares out the window as Griffin studies the map.

"I think it took us INSIDE the Bible," Griffin says.

"Wow," Lana breathes.

Griffin holds up the map. "Looks like our next stop is Mesopotamia."

"Mesopo-where?" Munch asks.

"Mesopotamia," Griffin repeats. "Sometimes it's called the Cradle of Civilization."

"And I think we're about to find out why," Lana says, pointing out the window.

MESOPOTAMIA

- Mesopotamia was the land between the Euphrates and Tigris Rivers. It is located in modern-day Iraq.
- The land in Mesopotamia had rich soil. Wheat, barley, fruits, and vegetables were grown there.
- People in this region also raised sheep, goats, and cattle.
- Mesopotamia is known as the Cradle of Civilization because the first settlements were here. The rivers allowed for easy travel and provided water for crops.
- Mesopotamia's climate is hot and dry, with little rainfall.
- The land is made up of plains, deserts, and mountains.
- Ancient Mesopotamian people lived in three-story houses. The lower level was used for animals. Extended families lived on the upper two levels. Grandmas, grandpas, moms, dads, aunts, uncles, cousins, and siblings all lived together.

The man and woman God made, Adam and Eve, live in the Garden of Eden. They are delighted with their home and with each other. They don't wear clothes, but they don't need to. They never feel embarrassed or lonely or angry or sad.

Adam and Eve are husband and wife and enjoy being together. After all, God made them for each other. They also love taking care of the plants and animals in the Garden. One day, while taking a long walk through the Garden, Adam asks his wife, "Have I ever told you how God made me?"

Eve smiles. "Tell me again," she says.

"He made me from the soil," Adam says. He leans down, scooping up a handful of brown dirt. "God used soil just like this to form my body, then he breathed life into me."

Eve leans against her husband. "And how did God make me?" she asks.

"God didn't want me to be alone," Adam says. "He brought me all the animals, one by one. I named them all—giraffe, zebra, aardvark, monkey, elephant. It was so much fun! But not one of them was right to be my partner." Adam takes Eve's hand and smiles. "So God put me into a deep sleep. Then he made you from one of my ribs."

"I'm glad we have each other," Eve replies.

Adam and Eve walk quietly for a while through the beautiful Garden. Adam stops to smell a flower. Eve pets a deer that walks up to greet her. They laugh when a flock of brightly colored pheasants bursts from a bush as they pass.

Finally, Adam and Eve reach the center of the Garden. They look up into the branches of the tall tree that grows there.

"God gave us this Garden to care for," Adam says. "And he also gave us a warning. He said we could eat from every tree in the Garden, except this one—the tree of the knowledge of good and evil."

Eve squeezes Adam's hand. "We will obey God's rule," she says. "We will not eat from this tree. Instead, we will eat from all the other trees and be happy with the animals, each other, and God—forever."

To learn more about Adam and Eve, read Genesis 2.

THINK ABOUT IT!

The man—Adam—named his wife Eve, because she would be the mother of all who live.

Genesis 3:20

Names in the Bible have special meaning. People were often given a name that reflected their character or role in life. The name *Adam* means "man," and the name *Eve* most likely comes from a Hebrew term that means "to give life." Do you know what your name means?

Off Course

One day, things go terribly wrong.

God's enemy, Satan, disguises himself as a snake and slithers into the Garden—right to the middle of it. There, he finds just who he is looking for: Eve, sitting near the tree of the knowledge of good and evil. Adam is napping, his head resting on Eve's lap.

The snake hisses at Eve.

"Hello, snake," Eve says. She squints at the scaly animal. "I'm sorry, but have we met? You don't look familiar. I thought I knew all the snakes in the Garden."

"I'm not like all the otherssss," the serpent hisses. "I'm ssspecial." He flicks his tail and creeps around the tree. "But enough about me. Let's talk about you." The serpent fixes his glinting eyes on the woman. "Poor Eve," he says. "Did God really say you can't eat the fruit from any of the beautiful trees in the Garden?"

"We may eat from all of the trees except this one," Eve replies. "God says that if we eat from the tree of the knowledge of good and evil or even touch it, we will die."

"Ssssilly," the snake hisses. "You won't die. God just doesn't want you to eat from this tree because then you will know all about good and evil—just like him."

Eve takes a good look at the fruit. Suddenly, it looks tastier than any of the other fruit she's enjoyed. And she really wants knowledge. So she reaches up and picks a ripened piece of fruit. She takes a bite, then shakes Adam awake and offers him some fruit.

"It's delicious," she says. "Try it." Adam also eats the fruit.

Instantly, Adam and Eve feel ashamed. They are suddenly embarrassed to be naked. They jump to their feet and scramble to cover themselves with leaves. Then they hear God's footsteps, coming closer and closer!

Adam and Eve leap behind some bushes to hide from God. Soon his footsteps sound right next to them.

"Adam, where are you?" God calls.

"We are hiding," Adam answers. "We are naked and afraid."

"Who told you that you were naked?" God asks. They have never heard his voice sound so sad. "Did you eat from the tree of the knowledge of good and evil?"

"Eve gave me the fruit," Adam says quickly. He has never said Eve's name that way before. She feels more ashamed than ever.

God turns toward Eve. "What have you done?" he says.

"It was the snake!" Eve cries. "He tricked me!"

God stops the snake as it tries to sneak away. "You are cursed because of what you have done," he tells it. "This is not the end of the story. One day, a descendant of this woman will strike your head, even though you strike him on the heel."

God looks sadly at Adam and Eve. "This is not what I wanted for you," he says. "Now your life will be hard. You will have to leave the Garden forever."

God makes clothing for Adam and Eve and sends them on their way. He places an angel at the entrance to the Garden. The angel holds a flaming sword to make sure that they can never return to Eden. God watches sadly as his children leave the beautiful home he built for them. Tears roll down Adam's and Eve's cheeks.

To learn more about the Fall, read Genesis 3.

BUILD YOUR FAITH!

Have you ever had a friend try to convince you to do something that you knew was wrong? What did you say to that person? How do you think Adam should have responded to Eve?

Terrible Good-byes

Adam and Eve learn how to live in a new and difficult world. They have to work hard to get food to eat. Sometimes they get sick. Sometimes they fight.

But there are still many beautiful things in the world. Adam and Eve still love each other. And God still loves them.

Soon Eve gets pregnant and has a baby boy. The birth is painful and scary, but she knows that God is by her side. She praises God for her new son, Cain. Some time later, Adam and Eve have another boy, Abel.

Cain grows up to be a farmer. He works the land, growing vegetables, fruit, and grain. Abel becomes a shepherd. He cares for a flock of sheep, taking them out in the field to snack on fresh grass.

One day near harvest time, the brothers decide to make offerings to God. Cain casually gathers some of his crops and tosses them into a basket to present to God. But he keeps back the very best fruit and vegetables and grain. "God doesn't eat this food," he says to himself. "We need it more than he does."

Abel looks carefully at all his firstborn lambs. He picks each one up and examines it from head to hoof. Finally he chooses the very best one. "God will surely be pleased with you," he says to the lamb. "You will be my offering to him."

Both brothers present their gifts to God. God is happy with Abel's lamb, but he is not pleased with Cain's crops. Cain stomps away, furious with God and his brother.

"Why are you so angry?" God asks Cain. "You will be accepted if you do what is right and give me your best. Be careful, because sin wants to control you. You must be the master over your sin." God knows that jealousy and sinful thoughts lurk inside Cain.

Cain cannot get control of his anger and jealousy toward his brother. Every day he grows more bitter that God accepted Abel's offering and not his. Finally, his sinful thoughts grow into a sinful plan. "Let's go for a walk in the fields," he says to Abel one afternoon. As the two brothers walk along, Cain suddenly attacks Abel and kills him. He returns home as if nothing has happened. But he can't fool God.

"Where is your brother?" God asks Cain.

"I don't know," Cain lies. "Is it my job to watch over him?"

"What have you done?" God asks. "Your brother's blood is crying to me from the earth. I know you killed him. Now you will be cursed and banned from the ground. The soil will no longer grow your crops. Instead, you will be a homeless wanderer."

"This punishment is too harsh!" cries Cain. "If I become homeless, everyone will try to kill me."

"No one will harm you," God says. "If they do, I will give them a worse punishment." God places a special mark on Cain to warn others not to hurt him. Feeling sorry for himself, Cain leaves. He makes a new home in the land of Nod, east of Eden.

To learn more about Cain and Abel, read Genesis 4.

A Very Long Cruise

"This is so sad!" Lana says, tears in her eyes. "Everything was so beautiful! Why did Adam and Eve have to disobey God?"

Wiping her eyes, Lana doesn't notice the thick mist that suddenly surrounds the bus. Munch and Griffin glance at each other curiously, but the mist disappears as quickly as it came. The kids can now see lots of people through the windows of the bus. "I think we traveled in time," Griffin murmurs. "Incredible!"

Munch frowns as he watches the people outside. "Yeah, Adam and Eve really messed up. And it looks like things are just getting worse and worse out there! Doesn't anyone care about following God anymore?"

"Look!" Griffin points out the window. "That man there, standing apart from everyone else. What's he doing?"

"He looks like he's thinking hard about something," Munch says.

"Or . . . maybe he's praying!" Lana says. "I bet that's Noah!"

The man is Noah. He is the only person left on the earth who cares about following God. He tries to do what is right and talks to God often. One day, God tells him something strange.

"I have a special job for you," God says. "I want you to build a large boat called an ark. Fill it with your family and two animals of every kind. I am going to send a massive flood to destroy the world. The flood will wash away all these evil people and the terrible things they have done."

Noah has never seen such a big boat; he can hardly even imagine it. But he does as God asks. He starts building right away. Day after day, the air is filled with the sounds of hammering and sawing. Noah works on the ark year after year after year.

When it is finally done, he stands back and marvels at the ark's enormous size—big enough to hold a male and a female of every kind of animal on the earth, as well as seven pairs of each type of bird and each animal to be used for food. God is pleased with the ark and with Noah's obedience and faith.

THINK ABOUT IT!

God said to Noah, ". . . Build a large boat from cypress wood."

Genesis 6:13-14

God gave Noah exact measurements for the ark. It was 450 feet long, 75 feet wide, and 45 feet high, and it had three levels, filled with stalls to hold all the animals (see Genesis 6:14-16). It was likely built very far away from any major body of water, like lakes or oceans. By building a huge boat with no water in sight, Noah was acting in faith—trusting that what God had told him would come true.

SLOW!

Soon God starts sending animals to Noah. Two by two they come and board the ark. There are horses, alligators, lions, parrots, and some that Noah can't even name. The animals form a line and enter the only door into the ark.

As raindrops start to fall, Noah calls for his family. He gathers his wife and his three sons, Shem, Ham, and Japheth. His sons' wives come too. They hug each other, say a prayer, and enter the ark. God closes the huge door behind them.

Giant raindrops start pounding on the roof and splashing against the windows of the bus. "We'd better get out of here, fast!" Munch shouts. The bus's engine roars, and they start moving along a dusty road.

"Hold on. It's about to get bumpy," Griffin says, looking at the road ahead. It winds up the side of a tall mountain and is covered with potholes.

"Where are we headed?" Munch asks.

"Mount Ararat," Griffin answers, pointing to a sign.

It rains and rains and rains. Soon, everything is underwater. "Nothing is left," Noah says, looking out the window at his changed world. The ark floats along in the raging water for months. Noah, his family, and the animals wait . . . and wait . . . and wait.

MOUNT ARARAT

- Mount Ararat is the highest mountain peak in Turkey. It is actually a sleeping volcano that last erupted in AD 1840.
- Nobody lives on Mount Ararat. Much of the mountain is covered in snow and ice.
- Summers on the mountain are warm, but winters can be very cold. There are also occasional snowstorms.

Fun Fact: The Bible says that Noah's ark landed on Mount Ararat after the great Flood. Many explorers have led expeditions to Mount Ararat looking for the ark. It has yet to be found. Many believe it is buried in the ice.

"Will we ever see dry land again?" Japheth wonders.

"Someday God will make the water go back down," Noah answers.

"Will our food run out?" Ham worries.

"God will provide for all our needs," Noah reassures him.

"When will we get off this ark?" Shem asks.

"God will tell us when the time is right," Noah says.

After five months . . . BUMP! People and animals are knocked off their feet. All of the animals cry out—horses neigh, wolves howl, and grizzly bears roar. Noah rushes to the railing. "We've landed on top of a mountain!" he shouts.

BUILD YOUR FAITH!

God made Adam and Eve responsible for all the animals he made (see Genesis 1:28). Later, Noah cared for God's animals while they were on the ark. We humans are still responsible for taking care of God's animals. How do you care for the animals in your life? If you have pets, do you remember to give them food, water, and a warm place to sleep? Even if you don't have a pet, there are things you can do to help the animals around you, like make a donation to or volunteer at a local animal shelter, or put up a birdhouse in your yard. Ask a trusted adult to help you brainstorm ways that you can do your part to take care of God's animals.

Everyone is excited, but they still can't leave the ark. The water is too high. Noah and his family wait some more. A few months later, Noah sends out a raven to search for dry ground. It flies back and forth but doesn't find anywhere to land. Next, Noah sends out a dove. This bird doesn't find dry ground either, so it comes back to Noah in the ark. A week later, Noah tries again. This time, the dove comes back with an olive leaf in its beak. Noah runs to show the leaf to his wife.

"This leaf is a sign that the land is almost dry!" Noah says. The next week he sends out the dove again. It doesn't come back to the ark. "The dove must have found a place to build its nest!" Noah tells his family. "We will get to leave the ark very soon."

But two more months go by. Noah and his family and the animals have been on the ark for more than a year. Every day, as they watch the earth dry out little by little, they get more impatient. Finally, one day God tells Noah, "It is safe to come out."

Everyone races for the door, pushing and shoving each other. When Noah steps outside, he sees a rainbow in the sky. "Look!" he says, pointing out the rainbow to his wife and sons and daughters-in-law. They marvel at the beautiful colors.

"This rainbow is the sign of my promise to you and all living creatures," God says. "I will never destroy the earth with a flood again."

Noah and his family worship God. Then they begin their new life in a world washed clean.

When I see the rainbow in the clouds, I will remember the eternal covenant between God and every living creature on earth.
Genesis 9:16

PARK HERE!
READ AND MEMORIZE THIS VERSE.

To learn more about Noah and the Flood, read Genesis 6–9.

An Unfinished Landmark

The bus engine rumbles to life again. "Are we turning around?" Lana asks. The bus loops around the peak of Mount Ararat and drives back down the same road it came up.

"It looks like we're heading back to Mesopotamia," Griffin says. "If I'm reading the map correctly—"

"If?" laughs Munch. "You've been reading maps correctly since before you could talk."

"If I'm reading the map correctly," Griffin repeats, ignoring Munch, "our next stop is Babylon."

"There's the sign!" Lana shouts, pointing out the window. "Babylon!"

Munch pulls out a squashed peanut-butter-and-jelly sandwich from his back pocket and takes a giant bite. Jelly splatters all over his shirt.

BABYLON

- Babylon was a wealthy and powerful city located near the Euphrates River, in modern day Iraq. It was the capital of Babylonia in southern Mesopotamia.
- Babylon was a grand city surrounded by huge walls. Adorned gates opened and led to the center of the city where a tall ziggurat stood. The king's palace was also in the center of the city.
- The Euphrates River was used for trading goods with other cities. The fertile soil near the riverbed allowed for crops, such as fruits and vegetables, to grow.
- Babylonians ate meat, fish, bread, fruits, and vegetables.
- Most houses were one story and made of clay brick. Only the wealthy had two-story homes. Clay was most often used for building because it was found along the river.
- The Hanging Gardens of Babylon, one of the Seven Wonders of the World, were thought to be located in the city, though archaeologists have not been able to find proof that the gardens existed.

Fun Fact: The ancient Babylonians were gifted mathematicians and astronomers. Math, science, astronomy, literature, and art flourished in the city of Babylon.

It is a hot and humid day in Babylon. The temperature soars and the sun beats down. Large groups of people are scurrying around a construction site. They are sweaty and tired, but they keep on working. They're building a tower. Workers form bricks out of clay and bake them in a fire. The bricks are lifted up the sides of the tower and placed on the top. The building grows taller by the hour.

"Our tower will be so high that it will reach all the way to heaven," one man brags.

"We will build the greatest city in the world!" another says.

"We will become famous! We can do anything!" The people's pride grows right along with the tower.

God overhears their bragging. "This

tower will make these people think that they do not need me anymore," he says. "I will confuse the languages of the people. They won't be able to understand each other, and the building will stop. Then I will scatter them all over the earth." So God makes the people start speaking different languages. Soon misunderstandings arise. It becomes too hard for them to work together. The people form small groups and scatter, leaving their unfinished tower.

To learn more about the tower of Babel, read Genesis 11:1-9.

THINK ABOUT IT!

[The people] said, "Come, let's build a great city for ourselves with a tower that reaches into the sky."

Genesis 11:4

The tower of Babel was most likely a *ziggurat*. A ziggurat is a tiered pyramid structure built on top of a platform. Ziggurats were religious buildings, built as part of a temple. The tower of Babel was probably made entirely out of mud or clay bricks.

The bus leaves Babylon and rumbles down the road. As the bus approaches a huge city, rain begins to fall. "Look at the storm clouds over the water," Lana says.

"That's the Persian Gulf," says Griffin. "I think we've arrived in Ur."

"Ur . . . what?" Munch asks.

"The name of the city is Ur," Griffin explains.

Munch snorts with laughter. "Urrr . . . Urrr . . ." he growls, baring his teeth at Lana and curling his fingers into claws.

"Stop it!" Lana shrieks, giggling.

The bus rolls to a stop next to a large, expensive-looking house. "Wow!" Griffin says, gawking out the window. "Who lives here?"

"Didn't Abram live in Ur?" Lana asks. "Maybe this is his house."

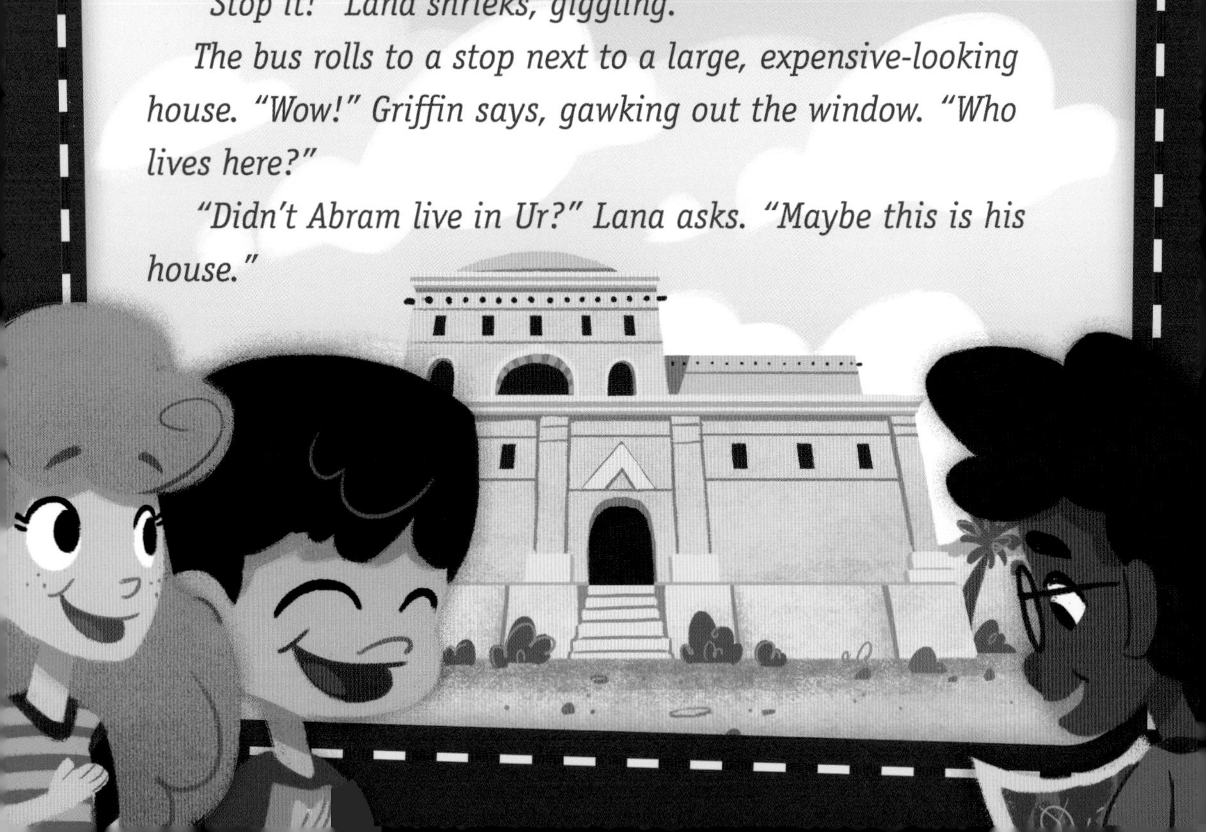

It is the home of Abram. Abram is gray haired and wears a well-made robe and sandals. He owns lots of gold and silver, as well as huge herds of animals. He has many servants to help him. He has a wife, Sarai, whom he loves very much. He has many relatives and is like a father to his nephew Lot. But one thing Abram does not have is a child of his own. Abram is seventy-five years old and Sarai is sixty-five, and they have never had a baby.

Abram loves and trusts God and often talks to him. God talks to Abram, too. One day, God gives Abram a surprising command. "Leave your home, country, and relatives," God says. "Go to the land I show you and settle there. I will give you many descendants, enough to make a great nation."

UR

- Ur was a city in the region of Sumer located in southern Mesopotamia (modern-day Iraq).
- Ur was situated where the Tigris and Euphrates Rivers meet the Persian Gulf.
- There are several cities named Ur. Scholars debate whether Abram and his extended family lived in northern Ur, north of Haran, or southern Ur.
- Ur was warm and dry with occasional rain. Summers were hot and winters were cold. Ur was prone to storms off of the Persian Gulf.

Fun Fact: From 1922 to 1934 a British archaeologist named Sir Leonard Woolley excavated the city of Ur. He discovered 16 royal tombs, many artifacts, and a mass tomb he called "The Great Death Pit." In the Great Death Pit were 74 bodies, mostly women. There were 6 male servants and 68 female servants wearing headdresses of gold. Overall, Woolley excavated approximately 1,850 burials. His 1922–34 excavation gave insight into what life was like in ancient Ur.

"God wants us to move away," Abram tells Sarai.

Sarai also trusts God. "All right," she says. "God knows what is best for us."

Husband and wife pack their clothing, food, and tents. They set out on a long and difficult journey. Their nephew Lot goes with them, and so do all of their servants. Abram and Lot each bring along all of their animals.

To learn more about Abram's big move, read Genesis 12:1-9.

"Look, another sign!" Munch says. He reads, "Canaan."

"Isn't this the land that God promised the Israelites?" Griffin asks.

"You're right, Griffin," Lana says.

"I think I remember that Abram is the ancestor of Israel," Griffin says. "But to be an ancestor, you have to have children. And Abram doesn't have any."

"He doesn't have any YET," Lana says. "Let's keep watching."

Sarai Tries a Shortcut

Year after year, Abram and Sarai pray for a child. And year after year, they are disappointed. The heartbreak is unbearable. *Why can't I have children?* Sarai asks God. *I want a son so much!* But God does not seem to be answering her prayers. Then one day, as Sarai is watching her young servant Hagar, she gets an idea.

Sarai rushes outside to find Abram.

"Abram," Sarai says, "we have prayed and prayed for a son, but I have never been able to have a baby. And now I am too old to get pregnant."

"Yes, I know," Abram says, looking at the ground.

"Well, I know how we can have a baby," Sarai says.

Abram looks up. "How?" he asks.

"You must have a baby with Hagar, my servant," Sarai explains. "I will raise the baby as my own. Maybe this is how God will keep his promise to give you descendants."

Abram agrees, and soon Hagar becomes pregnant.

At first, Sarai is thrilled that her plan seems to be working. But soon something unexpected happens. Hagar starts treating Sarai differently. She looks down on Sarai because she is able to have children and Sarai is not.

"Hagar is treating me horribly!" Sarai complains to Abram. "I can't take any more of this!"

"Well, she is your servant. Do whatever you think is best," Abram says. So Sarai takes all her shame and sadness and anger out on Hagar. Sarai is so unkind to her servant that Hagar decides to run away.

Hagar races through the wilderness to escape. She runs until she cannot go any farther. Exhausted, she stops at a stream for a drink. While Hagar is gulping water, the angel of the Lord appears! Hagar stares at the angel while water drips down her chin.

"Where are you going, Hagar?" the angel asks.

Abram believed the LORD, and the LORD counted him as righteous because of his faith.
Genesis 15:6

PARK HERE!
READ AND MEMORIZE THIS VERSE.

"I am running away from my mistress, Sarai," Hagar says. "She has been very cruel to me."

"You must return home to Sarai and treat her with respect," the angel tells Hagar. "You will have more descendants than you can count. You are pregnant with Abram's son. Soon, you will give birth to a baby boy, and you will name him Ishmael."

Hagar is surprised. *I can't believe that God would notice someone like me,* she says to herself. Thinking about her son, she returns home. Later that year, Hagar gives birth to baby Ishmael. Abram is 86 years old.

CANAAN

- Canaan was located between Babylon and Egypt, in modern-day Israel.
- Abraham moved to Canaan around 2091 BC. In Abraham's time, Canaanites were nomadic. This meant that they moved from place to place. They lived in tents made out of animal skins. They traveled by foot or rode donkeys. Donkeys were used to carry their belongings.
- Joshua led the Israelites to Canaan in 1422 BC. In Joshua's time, people settled in Canaan and stayed there. They grew crops and raised animals. Some of the crops they grew were barley, grapes, dates, figs, legumes, and cucumbers.

Fun Fact: The land of Canaan was also referred to as the Promised Land, because it was the land promised to Abraham and his descendants by God.

Abram is thrilled to have a son. But one night, God visits Abram and makes him a special promise. "I will give you more descendants than you can count," God tells Abram. "You will be the father of many nations! I will always be your God, and I will give the land of Canaan to you and your descendants forever."

Abram listens carefully as God tells him what to do to show that he and his family belong to God.

"I'm also changing your name," God continues. "From now on, I will call you Abraham, because you will be the father of many nations. And Sarai will now be called Sarah," God says. "I will bless her and make her the mother of nations."

Abraham still doesn't think that Sarah will ever have a baby. "Please give Ishmael your special blessing!" he says.

"I will bless Ishmael," God says. "But he is not the child of my promise. You and Sarah will have a child of your very own."

Abraham cannot believe his ears. *A child at our age? How could that happen?* he thinks.

"You will have a son and name him Isaac," God says. "I will bless both Isaac and Ishmael and make them into great nations."

"Thank you, God," Abraham says, falling to his knees.

To learn more about Hagar and Ishmael,
and God's promises to Abraham,
read Genesis 16–17.

No Shortcuts on God's Road

God is good to Abraham and Sarah, and he keeps his promise to them. When Abraham is 100 years old and Sarah is 90, Sarah gives birth to a baby boy. He is the child they always wanted and were so afraid they would never have. Abraham names the baby Isaac, which means "laughter." Sarah laughs with joy and delight, holding the precious child close against her chest. She has waited so long for this day. Rubbing her hand gently across the baby's back, she says to Abraham, "Can you believe God gave us this gift at our old ages?" Abraham wraps his arms tightly around Sarah and the baby. The new parents marvel at Isaac's beauty and God's goodness.

To learn more about the birth of Isaac, read Genesis 21:1-7.

A Hard Walk Uphill

The years pass, and Isaac grows into a strong, healthy boy. His parents love him more each day. They praise God every day for keeping his promise to them.

But one day, while Abraham is praying, thanking God again for his miracle son, God says something terrible. "Take your only son, Isaac, whom you love so much, and go to the land of Moriah. Kill Isaac as a sacrifice on one of the mountains that I will show you."

Abraham can't believe it. Why would God ask him to do such a horrible thing? Why would God give Abraham and Sarah a son after so many years and then just take him away? Didn't God promise that Isaac would become a great nation? But God doesn't say anything else.

Abraham stands still for a long time, his face in his hands. Finally, he takes a deep breath and lifts his head. "I have trusted God this far, and he has always been faithful," Abraham says to himself. "I will keep trusting him now."

The next morning, Abraham gets up early and gently shakes Isaac awake. "Son, get two of our servants," Abraham tells him. "God has asked us to travel to the top of a mountain to make an offering."

Isaac jumps out of bed and runs to find the servants. He is excited to go on a trip with his father. "Which mountain are we going to?" he asks.

"God will lead us to the right mountain," Abraham says. "It is in the land of Moriah."

"Won't we need wood for our trip?" Isaac asks.

"Yes, we will," Abraham says, picking up his axe.

Abraham and Isaac chop firewood for their journey. With the help of their servants, they load the logs onto the back of a donkey. Then Abraham, Isaac, and the two servants set out for the land of Moriah.

It's a long trip—three days of walking.

Every step is hard for Abraham. It feels like his feet are as heavy as stones. When they reach the base of a mountain, God sends Abraham a sign. "This is the place," Abraham says. He turns toward his servants. "Wait here," he tells them. "Isaac and I will go ahead alone. We'll meet up with you on our way back." The servants agree, finding a shady place to sit.

Abraham and Isaac walk quietly together for a while. Isaac seems to be wondering about something. Finally he speaks up. "Father," Isaac says, "I think we forgot something for our offering. We have fire and wood, but we forgot the sheep."

"Don't worry," Abraham says. "God will provide the sheep."

As Abraham approaches the place God has told him to go, he begins to cry. He quickly wipes away his tears so that Isaac doesn't see. Abraham builds an altar and places the wood on it. Then he ties Isaac up with rope and places him on top of the altar.

Abraham picks up his knife and holds it high. He closes his eyes, knowing what he must do next.

But then a voice cries out. "Abraham! Abraham!"

"Yes?" Abraham says. "I'm here!"

"Don't hurt the boy!" the voice says. It is the angel of the Lord! "You have proved that God is first in your life. You have not kept even your only son from him." Abraham drops his knife and quickly unties Isaac, pulling him into his arms.

Kissing his son, Abraham notices a ram behind Isaac's back. Its horns are tangled in the brush. "Isaac, look!" he says. Isaac and Abraham capture the ram. Tying it up, they place it on the altar and offer it to God. "Thank you, God, for providing for us," Abraham says.

After the sacrifice, Isaac and Abraham return to the place where their servants are waiting. Neither of them speaks about what happened on the mountain. They all travel home together. This time, Abraham's feet feel as light as air.

To learn more about Abraham's test, read Genesis 22.

Journey to Find a Wife

"Spinning sprockets," Munch mumbles. "Abraham sure had a lot of faith." Lana and Griffin nod.

The silence is broken by the sound of the engine. The bus makes a neat three-point turn and heads away from Canaan.

"Wait, where are we going?" Griffin asks, jumping up from his seat. "Abraham's story isn't over yet!"

The bus doesn't stop. Finally, a sign appears outside the window: "Aram-naharaim."

"Aram-na . . ." Munch tries to read the sign.

"Aram-naharaim," Lana says, looking at the Bible. "It's a land where Abraham lived for a while before reaching Canaan. Some of his relatives stayed there."

"But Abraham is long gone!" Munch says. "So what are WE doing back here?"

The bus comes to a screeching halt next to a well.

A man is standing near the well. His clothes are so covered with dust that it's impossible to tell what color they are. The man's face is tired and worried. He paces back and forth, then raises his eyes to heaven and starts to pray out loud.

"O Lord, God of my master, Abraham," he says, "you know that I promised to find a bride for Isaac here, in Abraham's homeland. Please show your love to my master by helping me find the right woman. I don't want to let Abraham and Isaac down."

Young women start coming to the well to draw water—short women, tall women, laughing women, and quiet women. The servant watches them for a while, then prays, "Here's what I need, God. I will ask one of these girls to give me a drink of water. If she says, 'Yes, have a drink, and I'll get water for your camels, too,' then I will know that she is the one you have chosen for Isaac." The servant takes a deep breath. "Here goes," he says, walking up to a young woman.

The girl is beautiful and carries a large water jug on her shoulder. She smiles shyly at Abraham's servant as he approaches her. "May I have a drink of water?" the servant asks.

The girl immediately lowers the jug into her arms and offers it to the servant. "Please have as much as you like, sir," she says. As soon

HARAN

- Haran is a city in the northwest part of Mesopotamia (modern-day Turkey).
- Haran is the city where Abram, Lot, and Sarai settled on the journey from Ur to Canaan.

Fun Fact: Haran is also known as Paddan-aram and Aram-naharaim.

as he hands the jug back, she says, "I'll get water for your camels, too." She runs back to the well and fills the jug with cold water. She pours the water into a trough so the camels can drink it, then goes back to refill the jug again and again, until the camels have had all the water they want. This is the sign the servant is looking for. He knows this woman will be the perfect wife for Isaac.

"Thank you, God," the servant whispers. "What is your name?" he asks the young woman.

"Rebekah," she replies.

The servant goes home with Rebekah and meets her family. He explains his mission and how God showed him that Rebekah is the woman he is looking for.

"Rebekah, will you travel back to the land of Canaan with me and marry my master's son?" the servant asks.

"Yes, I will," she says. With the blessing of her family, Rebekah sets off to meet her husband.

Isaac and Rebekah get married and fall in love. At first Rebekah is unable to have children, but eventually God allows her to get pregnant. "You are going to have twin boys," God tells Rebekah. "I will make two nations from their descendants."

When the boys are born, they don't look like twins at all. They don't even look like brothers! The older twin, Esau, is all red and has lots of hair. The younger boy, Jacob, has smooth skin and is born holding on to his brother's heel. As the boys grow up, their parents pick favorites. Isaac loves Esau best, while Rebekah favors Jacob.

To learn more about Isaac and Rebekah, read Genesis 24 and 25:19-28.

"Do you smell food?" Munch asks. "Because I do!" A giant growl rumbles from Munch's stomach and echoes throughout the bus. Griffin laughs.

"I think that's Jacob cooking," Lana says. "He's all grown up now!"

The smell of hot stew fills the tent. Esau bursts through the door. He is starving after a long day of hunting, and the aroma of the bubbling stew warms his stomach. "Give me some stew!" Esau roars at his brother, Jacob.

Esau and Jacob are very different from each other, and not just in appearance. Esau likes to hunt animals and be outside. Jacob prefers to stay indoors and spend time with his mother.

"I will give you some stew, if you give me your rights as the first son—your birthright," Jacob answers. Although he and Jacob are twins, Esau was born first. This gives him a special right to inherit his father's land.

"I am starving to death here!" Esau shouts. "I won't get to inherit anything if I die first!"

Jacob scoops some stew into a bowl and holds it just out of Esau's reach. "Promise me that I can have the birthright!" he says.

"Fine! I promise," says Esau. He grabs the stew and starts wolfing it down. Jacob hands him some bread to go with it. As Jacob watches his brother eat, a smile spreads across his face.

Years later, Isaac sits in darkness inside his tent. He has gone blind in his old age. Knowing that he will soon die, Isaac calls for his favorite son. He tells Esau, "Go hunting and prepare my favorite meal for me. After I eat, I will give you a special blessing." Rebekah overhears him. She wants her favorite son, Jacob, to receive the blessing instead.

"Listen to me, son," she says to Jacob. "Go and fetch two goats. I will use them to make your father's favorite meal. You can give it

THINK ABOUT IT!

[Jacob said to Esau,] "Trade me your rights as the firstborn son."

Genesis 25:31

Birth order was very important in Jacob and Esau's day. The firstborn son had special responsibilities. He was second in line to his father and therefore in charge of his younger siblings. When the father died, the firstborn son became head of the household. He received a larger inheritance than the other children. The firstborn son was responsible for taking care of his mother and his unmarried sisters, and made all of his family's important decisions.

SLOW!

to him, pretending to be your brother, and then you will receive the special blessing instead of Esau. Your father is too blind to notice the difference."

"But what if he touches me?" Jacob asks. "My skin is smooth, and Esau's skin is hairy."

"I will cover your arms with the skins of the goats," Rebekah says. "I will also give you your brother's clothing to wear."

Jacob agrees to his mother's trick. Shaking with nerves, he goes into his father's tent, carrying the special meal.

This is how I showed my love for you: I loved your ancestor Jacob, but I rejected his brother, Esau.

Malachi 1:2-3

"Is that you, my son?" his father asks.

"Yes, it's me, Esau," Jacob says.

"That's strange—you sound like Jacob," Isaac says. "Come closer."

Certain that he is about to be discovered, Jacob fearfully approaches his father. But the hairy goatskins and the smell of Esau's clothes convince Isaac. He gives Jacob his blessing. Shortly afterward, Esau returns from hunting. He prepares his father's favorite meal and delivers it to him, anxious for his blessing. "But I already gave the blessing to your brother!" Isaac cries. "I thought it was you!" Isaac realizes he has been deceived. "I cannot take the blessing back," Isaac says to Esau. "Now you will serve Jacob forever."

Esau is furious. He feels nothing but hatred for his brother. "Soon my father will die," he says to himself. "When that happens, I will kill Jacob."

Rebekah knows what Esau is thinking. Fearing for Jacob's life, she quickly makes another plan. "Please send Jacob back to my family to find a wife," she says to Isaac. "I don't want him to marry a girl from around here." Isaac agrees and tells Jacob to go visit his uncle Laban, Rebekah's brother.

BUILD YOUR FAITH!

Jacob was unkind to Esau. Were you ever unkind to a sibling or a friend? In what ways could Jacob have been kinder to his brother? How do you make things right with a friend whom you have hurt?

To learn more about Jacob and Esau, read Genesis 25:29-34 and 27:1–28:5.

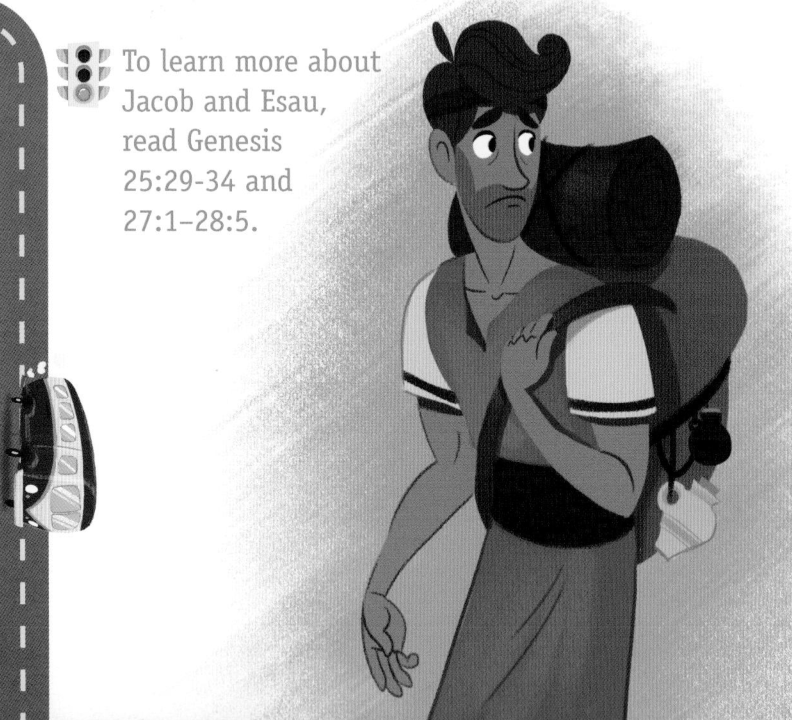

Too Many Trips to Dreamland

Trickster Jacob meets his match in his uncle Laban. Jacob falls in love with Laban's younger daughter, Rachel, but Laban tricks him into marrying Rachel's older sister, Leah, before allowing him to marry Rachel as well. The two sisters spend years competing for Jacob's love.

Like his mother and father, Jacob plays favorites with his children. He has twelve sons, but he loves Joseph, Rachel's first son, more than any of the others. When Rachel dies while giving birth to her second son, Benjamin, Jacob feels that Joseph is more precious to him than ever. He gives Joseph a special gift to show how much he loves him. Joseph opens the present. "It's wonderful!" cries Joseph, trying on the beautiful coat. "It has all the colors of the rainbow. I will wear it everywhere I go."

Jacob's other sons are jealous of the gift. They don't like the special attention that Joseph gets. "Why does he get a special coat?" they wonder.

Things get worse when Joseph starts having dreams. "I dreamed that we were all tying grain into bundles," he tells his brothers. "Then my bundle stood up straight and all of yours bowed down to it."

"Joseph thinks he is better than us," his brothers mutter to each other. "Does he really think he will be our king someday?"

Another day, Joseph tells his family, "Listen to what I dreamed last night! The sun, moon, and eleven stars bowed down to me!"

This time, even Jacob thinks that Joseph has gone too far. "What kind of dream is that?" he scolds his son. "Do you really think the whole family should come and bow to you?" But Jacob wonders what these dreams could mean.

Joseph likes to check up on his brothers and tell his father what they are doing. One day, the brothers take their father's sheep far away. "Go see what your brothers are up to," Jacob tells Joseph.

Joseph sets out right away. His brothers see him coming from a distance.

"There's that dreamer, coming to check up on us," Levi groans.

"I am so tired of hearing him talk about himself!" Zebulun says.

"I'm tired of watching our father treat him like the prince of our family," Asher grumbles. "I wish he would just go away."

The brothers look at each other. “Maybe that could be arranged,” Simeon says. The others begin to smile.

“Hold on,” says Reuben, the oldest. “We can’t kill our own brother!” He points to a big hole in the ground. “Let’s just throw him in this empty well. He’ll die out here without us having to actually kill him.” Reuben secretly plans to come rescue Joseph once everyone else has gone home.

The brothers agree to Reuben’s plan, and they throw Joseph into the hole. Joseph cries out when he reaches the bottom.

“What’s wrong?” his brothers say. “Can’t you DREAM up a way out?” They laugh.

Reuben leaves, and the rest of the brothers sit down to eat.

Suddenly, Judah spots a caravan of camels passing by. "Traders!" he says. "Let's sell Joseph to them! Then we can get rid of him and make some money, too!" The brothers agree, and soon the sale is made. The traders disappear into the desert, dragging Joseph behind them. The sound of his crying fades away.

"We won't have to worry about Joseph anymore," Naphtali says. "Those traders are headed to Egypt."

When Reuben gets back, he is upset at what his brothers have done. But he agrees to help them cover up their crime.

At home, Jacob cannot figure out why Joseph hasn't returned. "Where is my son?" he asks.

"Joseph must have been eaten by wild animals," his other sons lie. "We found his coat covered in blood."

Jacob is heartbroken. His family tries to comfort him, but he won't stop mourning the loss of his favorite son.

To learn more about Joseph and his brothers, read Genesis 37.

"I don't need the map to know where we are going next," Griffin says.

"Egypt, here we come!" Munch and Griffin shout together.

EGYPT

- Egypt is a very old country located in northeast Africa.
- The Nile River flows through Egypt. It is the longest river in the world. Every year, the Nile River would flood. The flooding produced rich soil good for growing crops.
- Ancient Egyptians grew wheat, barley, fruits, and vegetables. They also ate fish, sheep, and waterfowl.
- Most of Egypt is a sandy desert, with a very hot and dry climate. There are only two seasons: summer and winter. Winters in Egypt are warm with occasional rain.
- Ancient Egyptian homes were two- or three-room houses made out of mud bricks. Mud was often used as a building material because it could be found along the riverbed. Sometimes wealthy people built their houses out of stone.

Fun Fact: The Great Pyramid of Giza, located in Egypt, was standing during the time of Joseph. So he would have seen one of the Seven Wonders of the World.

When Joseph arrives in Egypt, an Egyptian officer named Potiphar buys him from the traders to be his servant. It isn't long before Potiphar realizes that Joseph is special. God makes Joseph successful in everything he does. "Joseph is a hard and loyal worker," Potiphar tells his wife. "Look at how well he accomplishes his tasks. I am going to put him in charge of running everything I own." Joseph manages Potiphar's home and property with wisdom and skill. Potiphar is very impressed with Joseph's abilities. But Potiphar's wife is impressed with Joseph's good looks. Soon, she begins to think he is more handsome and more interesting than her own husband. She starts following him around as he does his work. One day, she tells Joseph how she feels.

"I could never think of you in that way," Joseph says. "You are my master's wife. Potiphar trusts me with everything, except you. You belong only to him."

But Potiphar's wife will not give up. He tries to avoid her, but one day she finds him alone in the house. "Come with me, Joseph!" she cries, grabbing him.

"No!" Joseph shouts, tearing himself away from her. He runs out of the house, leaving his cloak in her hands.

Potiphar's wife realizes that Joseph

will never return her feelings for him. This makes her furious. Gripping his cloak in both hands, she screams for her servants. Soon, they come running from all directions. "Look!" she yells, shaking Joseph's cloak at them. "Joseph tried to attack me!"

When Potiphar gets home, she tells him the same story. Enraged at the thought that Joseph would betray his trust, Potiphar has him thrown in prison.

"I didn't do anything!" Joseph protests as guards hurl him into a prison cell. He lands on the ground with a loud thud. Rubbing his head, he looks around at the damp and dirty surroundings. “I didn’t do anything,” he says once more. The guards lock the door to his cell.

Soon, the warden of the prison also notices that the Lord is with Joseph. The warden puts Joseph in charge of all the other prisoners.

Once again, Joseph proves that he is a hard and loyal worker.

Some time later, new prisoners come to the jail. They are the chief cup-bearer and chief baker of Pharaoh, the king of Egypt. One day, Joseph notices that they look upset. "Why are you so worried?" he asks them.

"I had the weirdest dream last night," the cup-bearer says. "I just don't understand it."

"I had a strange dream too," says the baker. "Can anyone tell us what these dreams mean?"

"With God's help, I can explain the meaning of dreams," Joseph says to the men. The men tell Joseph the details of their dreams. The cup-bearer dreamed of a grapevine with three branches. First buds, then flowers, then grapes appeared on the branches. The cup-bearer took a cluster of grapes from the vine and squeezed their juice into Pharaoh's cup. Then he took the cup to Pharaoh and put it in his hand.

"Here's what your dream means," Joseph says. "The three branches represent three days. In three days, you will be released from prison, and you will go back and work for Pharaoh as his chief cup-bearer. When that happens, will you please mention me to Pharaoh?" Joseph asks. "I do not belong in prison, because I have not committed any crimes." Thrilled at the good news, the cup-bearer promises to tell Pharaoh about Joseph.

"My turn!" says the baker. After hearing such a good interpretation of the cup-bearer's dream, he is excited to hear what his might mean.

"I dreamed that I had three baskets of delicious pastries for Pharaoh stacked on my head. Then birds came and started eating the pastries out of the baskets."

Joseph looks at the baker with sadness. "I am very sorry," he says. "The three baskets in your dream also represent three days. But in three days, Pharaoh will have you killed."

Both of Joseph's predictions come true. Three days later, the baker is killed and the cup-bearer goes back to work for Pharaoh. Once the cup-bearer is back in the palace, he forgets all about his promise to Joseph.

Two years later, Pharaoh wakes up in a grumpy mood. "Where is my breakfast?" he yells. "Where are my servants? Why isn't anyone working around here?"

Pharaoh calls for all his wise men and magicians. "I hardly got any sleep last night," he grumbles at them. "I had two very upsetting dreams. Tell me what they mean." But not a single one of them has any idea what the dreams mean.

More annoyed than ever, Pharaoh calls for a drink. The cup-bearer hurries in. "Forgive me, your majesty," he says. "Today I remembered something very important. Back when I was in prison with the chief baker, we both had strange dreams. There was a young man in the prison who told us what they meant. I think he might be able to help you."

Minutes later, a guard shows up at Joseph's cell. There is a sound of jingling metal as he takes out a key and unlocks the door. *Creak!* The door swings open. "Pharaoh has requested your presence," he tells Joseph. Joseph is confused but follows the guard to the palace.

"I heard you know all about dreams," Pharaoh says to Joseph.

"Not really," Joseph says, "but God does."

Pharaoh tells Joseph his dreams. "I dreamed that seven fat cows were eating grass by the Nile River. Then seven skinny cows came along and ate the seven fat cows. Then, I dreamed that there was a stalk with seven heads of healthy grain. Seven weak and unhealthy heads of grain appeared. The wind blew and the unhealthy grain swallowed up the healthy grain."

"Both of your dreams mean the same thing," Joseph explains. "God is telling you that there will be seven years when crops will produce more food than usual. After that, there will be a great famine—seven years when the crops will not grow."

"What should I do?" Pharaoh asks.

THINK ABOUT IT!

The seven years of famine began, just as Joseph had predicted. The famine also struck all the surrounding countries, but throughout Egypt there was plenty of food.

Genesis 41:54

Joseph predicted that Egypt would experience a famine. A famine happens when an area does not produce enough food. Famines can occur because of bad weather that harms the crops, war or fighting, too many people living in an area, or food starting to cost too much for people to be able to buy it. Famines have happened in almost every country. Some countries, such as Somalia and South Sudan, are experiencing famines today.

"Find someone who is wise and put him in charge of Egypt," Joseph suggests. "Appoint leaders to store away some extra grain so that no one will starve during the famine."

Pharaoh stares at Joseph for a few moments. He finally speaks. "I don't know anyone wiser than you," Pharaoh says. "Obviously, the Lord is with you. I am making you my second-in-command. You will answer only to me." Pharaoh turns to his officials and the other members of his court. "All of you, do whatever Joseph tells you," he says. Pharaoh gives Joseph his signet ring to wear to show that Joseph speaks for him. He also gives him the finest Egyptian clothes and jewelry to wear. In one day, Joseph has gone from prisoner to prince.

The Egyptians hang on Joseph's every word and do whatever he tells them. For seven years they store the extra food that grows in the fields. Then the seven years of famine begin. No rain falls, and no crops grow. The famine spreads throughout Egypt and the lands around it. "We're running out of food," an Egyptian official tells Joseph. "What should we do?"

"It's all right," Joseph replies. "We have stored plenty of grain." Joseph stands before the people, easing their worries.

"We even have enough food to sell to people from other lands," Joseph reassures the Egyptians. "Nobody will starve."

People come from all over to buy food from Joseph. One day, Joseph sees a group of 10 men approaching. He instantly recognizes them as his brothers. The men kneel before Joseph. Joseph can hardly believe it—his dreams from so long ago have come true!

But his brothers do not recognize him. "Please help us," they plead. "We come from the land of Canaan, where we have run out of food. Our family is starving."

"You are probably spies," Joseph says to them. "You are here to see if you can attack our land."

"No!" the brothers insist. "There are 12 of us brothers, the sons of Jacob, and we live in Canaan. Our youngest brother, Benjamin, is back home with our father, and one of our brothers is gone forever. We came to Egypt looking for food. We are not spies."

[Joseph said,] "You intended to harm me, but God intended it all for good. He brought me to this position so I could save the lives of many people."
Genesis 50:20

Joseph agrees to sell food to them, but he doesn't tell them who he really is. He fills their sacks with grain but secretly puts the money they paid him back in the sacks. "Prove to me that you are not spies," Joseph says to his brothers. "Go home and get your youngest brother, Benjamin, and bring him back here. Until you do, I will keep one of you here as prisoner." He chooses Simeon and ties him up.

"We are being punished for selling Joseph to the slave traders," the brothers whisper to one another. They return to Canaan and tell their father what has happened. They are even more afraid when they find the returned money in their sacks.

It takes a lot of convincing, but Jacob finally agrees to allow Benjamin to return with his brothers to Egypt. "If you do not come back home with Benjamin, then I will die of a broken heart," their father says. "I've already lost Joseph. I can't stand to lose Benjamin, too."

The brothers return to Egypt with Benjamin. When Joseph sees them, he invites them to a great feast at his house. They eat lots of delicious food. But then Joseph plays another trick on the brothers. Before sending them on their way, he fills each of their sacks with grain and returns their money to their sacks, just like before. Then he places his fine silver cup inside the bag that belongs to Benjamin.

Joseph's brothers tell him good-bye and start on their journey back to Canaan. But when they are barely outside the city walls, Joseph's palace manager catches up to them. "Stop!" he calls. "One of you has stolen my master's silver cup."

"We would never do such a thing," the brothers protest.

The manager searches their bags and finds the silver cup inside Benjamin's bag. "You thief!" the palace manager says. "You will stay here and be Joseph's slave. The rest of you may go free."

"No!" the brothers cry. They all go back with the palace manager to Joseph's house.

Judah explains to Joseph that if they do not return home with Benjamin, their father will die of a broken heart. "I promised my father that I would keep Benjamin safe," he tells Joseph. "Please let me stay and be your slave in his place."

Joseph can't take it any longer. He sends all of his servants out of the room and starts to cry loudly. "I am Joseph!" he tells his brothers. He weeps and kisses each of them. The brothers cannot believe it. "Don't be sad about what you did," Joseph tells them. "God sent me here to Egypt. It was his plan so that I could save your lives during this famine.

BUILD YOUR FAITH!

God helped Joseph to forgive his brothers. Forgiveness is not always easy. Have you ever had a hard time forgiving someone who hurt you? Forgiveness takes faith. If we want God to forgive us for our sins, then we must learn to forgive others who wrong us.

Now go and get our father. Come to Egypt to live. Bring along all of your families."

The brothers run home to tell their father the good news. "Joseph is alive!" Jacob shouts with joy. "Let's go to Egypt so that I may see him once more." Joseph's father, brothers, and all of their families move to Egypt. Pharaoh is kind to them and gives them good land to live in.

God gives Joseph a kind and forgiving heart. "Don't worry," Joseph tells his brothers. "God took the evil you did to me and turned it into good. He made it possible for me to save the lives of many people—including yours!"

To learn more about Joseph, read Genesis 37 and 39–50.

A sandstorm blows up from the desert, rocking the bus and hiding the view out the windows.

"What's happening?" Munch shouts, holding tightly to the seat in front of him.

Lana has her face buried in the Bible. She doesn't seem to notice the bus rocking.

"Joseph and his family have many good years together in Egypt," she says. "They have many descendants, who become known as the Hebrews, or Israelites. But then, a new Pharaoh comes along, and he doesn't remember Joseph."

"The new Pharaoh is really cruel," Griffin adds, reading over Lana's shoulder. "He makes the Hebrews his slaves."

Munch looks around nervously. He is relieved when the sand clears from the windows, revealing a huge river.

"That must be the Nile!" Lana says.

A little girl hides in the tall grass near the Nile River. She doesn't take her eyes off a basket that floats gently down the river, among the reeds near the shore.

Hours ago, the girl's mother wove that basket out of grass and covered it with tar to keep the water out. She placed the girl's baby brother into the basket and set it afloat in the Nile. The girl knew that her mother was doing this to save the baby's life.

"Watch your little brother's basket, Miriam," the girl's mother told her. Tears ran down her mother's face, making it hard for her to speak. "Don't let him out of your sight! Follow along the river until you see what happens to him."

Miriam hears voices and crouches lower in the grass. "Find all the baby boys!" an Egyptian soldier shouts. "We cannot miss a single one! Pharaoh wishes to get rid of them all!" Miriam hears footsteps close by. She squeezes her eyes shut, holds her breath, and prays that the baby will not cry.

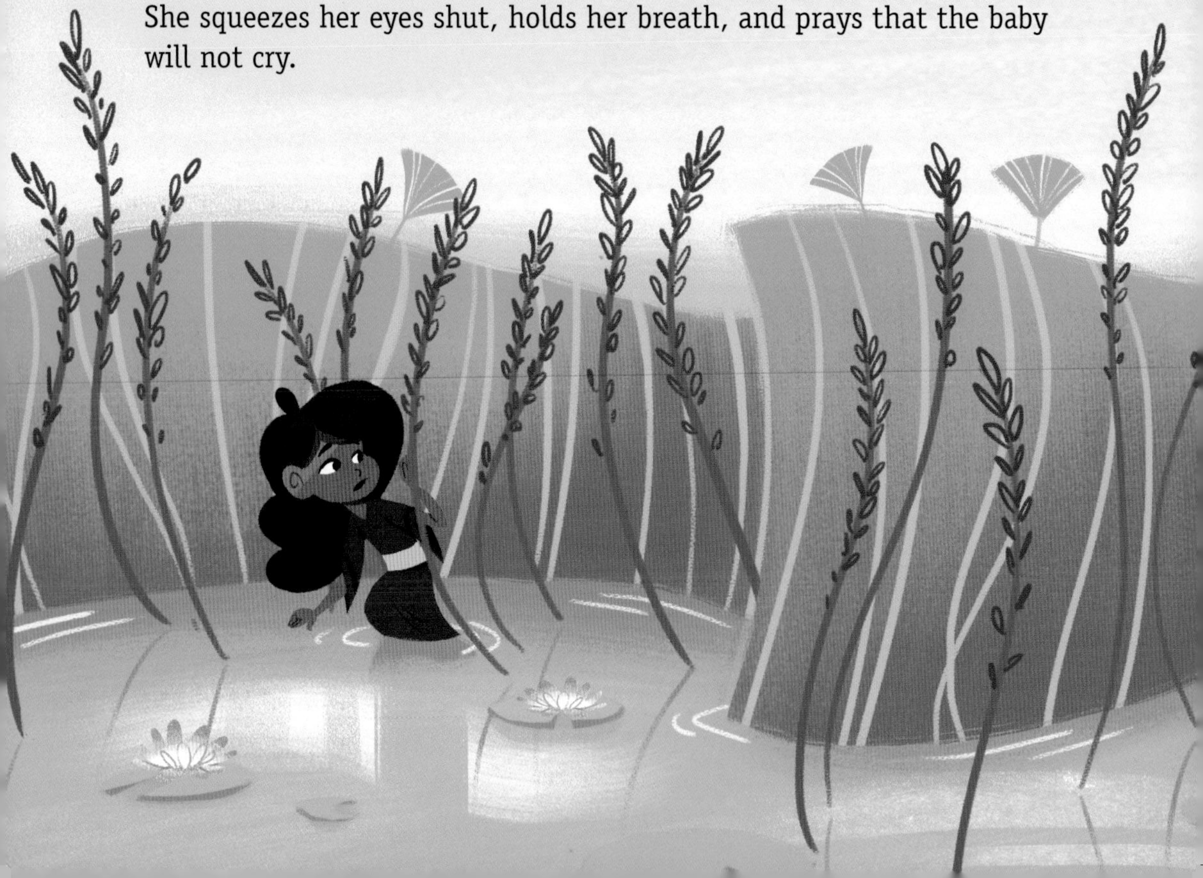

Splashing nearby makes Miriam's eyes open wide. Have the soldiers spotted the basket? Are they going into the river to hurt the baby? Instead, Miriam is stunned to see a beautiful princess.

Pharaoh's daughter has come to the river to bathe. She splashes and laughs with her maids. Then she catches sight of something in the reeds. "What is that?" the princess asks, pointing to the basket. She tells one of her maids to bring it to her.

Miriam presses her hands to her mouth to keep from crying out. Surely the princess has heard her father's orders. Will she take the baby to him to be killed?

The princess opens the basket and gasps. "It's a baby!" she exclaims. The baby boy looks up at her and smiles. The princess immediately falls in love with him. She lifts him out of the basket and holds him close. "This must be one of the Hebrew babies," she tells her maids. "But he is mine now. I am going to keep him, and I will name him Moses."

Miriam can hardly believe her ears! Trembling, she steps out of the grass and approaches the princess. "I can find a Hebrew woman to nurse the baby for you," she suggests.

"Good idea!" the princess says. "Tell the woman I will pay her for her help."

Miriam runs to get her mother. Both of them cry with joy as Miriam tells her what has happened. They hurry back to the princess. That night, baby Moses sleeps in his own bed again. God has not only saved his life, but also allowed his own mother to take care of him!

To learn more about baby Moses, read Exodus 2:1-10.

Desert Round-Trip

The bus drives away from the Nile River, into the desert.

"Moses' mother took care of him until he was older, then brought him to Pharaoh's palace to be raised by the princess," Lana explains.

"You mean Moses grew up as the son of Pharaoh's daughter?" Griffin asks.

"Spinning sprockets!" Munch says. "Moses went from slave to prince!"

"That's right," Lana says. "But God had even bigger plans for Moses than being a prince." The bus drives past a sign that reads "Midian."

MOUNT SINAI

- Mount Sinai is located on the Sinai Peninsula in Egypt. It is is 7,497 feet tall and surrounded by other mountain peaks.
- Summers are hot and dry with cool nights. Winters are full of rain.
- Few animals can be seen on the mountain, but occasionally a fox, eagle, wildcat, or hedgehog can be seen.
- Today it is possible to hike to the top of the mountain. Along the way to the summit some chapels have been built.

Fun Fact: Scholars disagree on whether the place we know as Mount Sinai is the same as the biblical Mount Sinai.

MIDIAN

- Midian is located in the northwest region of the Arabian Desert, in modern day Saudi Arabia.
- Midianites were nomadic, meaning they traveled from place to place.
- Midianites had cattle and camels. They engaged in caravan trading.

Fun Fact: Some scholars claim Midian was not a geographical place but a group of tribes that came together for worship.

Moses no longer lives in Egypt, and he is no longer a prince. He ran away from home after killing an Egyptian in order to protect a Hebrew slave. Moses ran to the land of Midian, where he joined the household of a priest named Jethro. Moses married Jethro's daughter Zipporah and had two sons of his own. He became a shepherd and nearly forgot about the people in Egypt.

One day, Moses leads some sheep into the wilderness to graze. The sheep nibble on grass and roam the open space. They go all the way to Mount Sinai, the mountain of God. While he is watching his flock, Moses sees something burning brightly. He approaches it to get a better look. It's a bush in flames. "The bush is on fire, but it is not burning up," Moses says to himself. He has never seen anything like this before. As Moses walks closer to the bush, he hears someone call out his name.

"Moses! Moses!" the voice says.

"Here I am!" Moses answers.

"Take off your sandals," says the voice. "Because the ground you are standing on is holy. I am the God of your ancestors Abraham, Isaac, and Jacob."

Moses immediately takes off his sandals to show respect for this place where God is.

"I have not forgotten how much my people are suffering in Egypt," God says. "I am about to rescue them from slavery. I will lead them to a new land, a good one where they will be safe and have all that they need."

This all sounds good to Moses. But then God says, "You will lead my people, Moses. I want you to go to Pharaoh and tell him to let my people go."

"Me?" Moses asks. "Why would you pick me to do this?"

"I will be with you, Moses," God says.

"But if I go to the people and tell them that God sent me," Moses says, "they will ask me who you are. What do I tell them your name is?"

"Tell them that I am who I am," God says. "Tell them that I am Yahweh, the God of your ancestors."

"But what if they don't believe me?" Moses asks.

"What have you got in your hand?" God responds.

Moses looks down at the staff in his hand. The wood feels smooth under his fingers. "It's my shepherd's staff," he answers.

"Throw it on the ground," God says. Moses hurls his staff onto the ground. When the staff touches the earth, it transforms into a hissing snake. Moses jumps away from it.

"Now reach out and pick up the snake by its tail," God says. Moses knows that it is usually a very bad idea to grab a snake's tail. But he obeys God and picks it up. As soon as he lifts it, the snake turns back into a staff.

Then God gives Moses another sign. "Take your hand and place it inside your clothing," he says. Moses looks at his hand and places it inside his cloak. "Now remove your hand," God orders. When Moses pulls his hand back out, it is covered with a skin disease. Moses cries out in panic. "Put your hand back into your cloak," God tells him. When Moses pulls his hand out a second time, it is healthy.

"If the people do not believe that I sent you," God says, "show them those two signs. And if they do not believe you after that, then take water from the Nile River. Pour it onto the ground. The water will turn into blood."

Moses still doesn't want this job. "God, I'm no good at speaking. When I try to talk to people, my tongue gets all tied up in knots!"

"Moses," God says, "who makes mouths and tongues? Who gives people the ability to talk in the first place? That's right—me. Now get going! I will tell you what to say."

"Please, please, please send someone else!" Moses begs.

God gets angry with Moses. "Listen. I will send your brother, Aaron, with you. He will speak for you. I will tell you both what to say and do."

Moses finally agrees to go to Egypt. He tells his wife and sons to pack up their belongings. Aaron, Moses' older brother, meets him near Mount Sinai. Together, they set off to see Pharaoh.

To learn more about Moses and the burning bush, read Exodus 3–4.

Pharaoh's U-Turns

The bus starts up and turns around. "And it's back to Egypt again," Griffin says.

"I can't wait to see what Pharaoh does when Moses shows him his staff-snake!" Munch says. "God's inventions are the coolest."

Lana laughs. "Look—there's Pharaoh."

Pharaoh is not impressed with Moses and Aaron, or with their request, or even with their God. "I have never heard of this God," Pharaoh says, looking down his nose at the roughly dressed men standing before him. "I see no reason why I should let MY slaves go."

Pharaoh is so angry at Moses and Aaron that he gives orders that the Israelite slaves should be worked even harder. They will no longer be given straw to make bricks with, but they will have to make the same number of bricks as before. The people are devastated—then they get angry with Moses and Aaron too.

"Why did you even come?" they demand. "You're making things worse for us!"

Moses cries out to God. "Didn't you send me here, God?" he asks. "Didn't you tell me to come? Why are things getting worse instead of better?"

God tells Moses and Aaron to go before Pharaoh again. "Prove that your God is real!" Pharaoh dares them. "Show me a miracle!"

Moses nods to Aaron, who throws his staff down on the ground. The staff becomes a snake, just like it did on Mount Sinai when God spoke to Moses out of the burning bush.

"That's nothing!" Pharaoh scoffs. He snaps

THINK ABOUT IT!

The slave drivers and foremen went out and told the people: "This is what Pharaoh says: I will not provide any more straw for you. Go and get it yourselves. Find it wherever you can. But you must produce just as many bricks as before!"

Exodus 5:10-11

The Israelites used mud bricks for building. They got the mud from the Nile River. But a brick made entirely out of mud is weak, so straw was usually added to the mud when the bricks were formed. The straw would help the mud dry faster and would increase the strength of the brick once it was baked in the sunlight.

his fingers, and his court magicians also throw staffs onto the ground. Their staffs become snakes too!

Aaron's staff-snake slithers over to the Egyptian snakes. It hisses and unhinges its jaw, opening its mouth wide. Then Aaron's snake swallows up the snakes made by the magicians! But Pharaoh still will not let God's people go.

"Pharaoh has a stubborn heart," God tells Moses. "It's time for me to show him that only I am God."

Following God's instructions, Moses meets Pharaoh in the morning on the bank of the Nile River.

"This is what you get for not listening to God," Moses tells Pharaoh. Aaron raises his staff up high, then hits the river water with it. Suddenly the river water turns into blood!

Across Egypt, people gasp and scream as all of their water—in rivers, streams, ponds, wells, and even jugs and pitchers—turns into blood. A horrible smell spreads across Egypt. There is no water left to drink.

"God warned you," Moses says to Pharaoh. "Let his people go."

"Never!" Pharaoh says. He goes home and tries to forget about God, while his people frantically dig wells, looking for clean water.

A week later, Moses and Aaron go to see Pharaoh again.

"Let God's people go!" they say.

"No!" Pharaoh responds.

"You're bringing this on yourself," Moses says. "Raise your staff again, Aaron."

Aaron raises his staff again, and God sends a second plague. Croaking fills the air.

"What is that awful sound?" Pharaoh asks, covering his ears. He soon gets his answer. Frogs are everywhere. They cover the ground and hop into the Egyptians' homes. Frogs cover every surface, getting into people's beds and food. A huge frog jumps into Pharaoh's lap. He yells in disgust, then speaks to Moses and Aaron.

"Fine!" Pharaoh shouts. "I will let your people go. Just get rid of the frogs!"

"Tell me when," Moses says.

"Tomorrow!" Pharaoh replies.

God causes all the frogs to die at once the next day. Huge piles of dead, stinking frogs appear all over Egypt. When Pharaoh sees that the plague is gone, he changes his mind and does not let the people go.

"Time for another plague," God tells Moses. Aaron strikes the ground with his staff. The dust turns into a plague of gnats that cover the Egyptians and their animals.

"These plagues are definitely the work of God!" Pharaoh's magicians tell him. Pharaoh ignores them.

Next, flies swarm the Egyptians. But there is not a single fly to be found in Goshen, the area where the Israelites live.

"Make it stop!" says Pharaoh. "I will release the slaves."

"You'd better not be lying again," Moses says. He prays to God, and the flies go away. But Pharaoh changes his mind again. So God kills all of the Egyptians' livestock—their horses, donkeys, camels, cattle, sheep, and goats—all the animals they rely on for food and clothing and farm work. Pharaoh sends some men to Goshen to see what has happened to the Israelites' animals. Not one Israelite animal has even gotten sick. But Pharaoh stays stubborn.

Then the Egyptians themselves get sick. Their bodies are covered in painful sores. But Pharaoh grits his teeth and stays stubborn.

"God is going to send hail!" Moses tells Pharaoh. "You'd better get your people and animals under cover."

"I'm not afraid of a little hail," Pharaoh sniffs. But some of his officials have seen enough. They quickly bring their servants and animals in from the fields. And just in time. Hail falls from the sky in giant chunks. It damages the Egyptians' homes and chariots. It destroys the crops in their fields. It even kills people and animals.

"All right, I'll let you go!" Pharaoh says. But he still doesn't mean it. When the hail stops, he changes his mind yet again.

"Locusts are next!" Moses tells Pharaoh.

"Please listen to him!" Pharaoh's officials beg. "Let the slaves go, or Egypt will be destroyed!" But Pharaoh stays stubborn, and locusts eat all of the remaining crops and every blade of grass.

"I'm sorry," Pharaoh says to Moses and Aaron. "Please ask God to forgive me and take away these horrible locusts."

Moses prays to God, and God sends a strong wind that blows every single locust away.

And Pharaoh changes his mind AGAIN.

So God sends a great blackness over the land. For three days, it is so dark that the Egyptians can't even move.

"This is your last chance, Pharaoh," Moses says. "The final plague will be the worst. If you don't let us go now, the firstborn son in each Egyptian family will die."

But Pharaoh still does not want to listen. "Get out of here!" he screams at Moses and Aaron. "I will kill you if I see your faces again!" So Moses and Aaron go home.

"Listen carefully," God says to Moses. "Tell all the Israelites to sacrifice a lamb or goat and mark their doors with the animal's blood. I will pass over the doors with the special marking and will not kill the firstborn sons in those homes. You will have a celebration on this day every year from now on to remember the night that I freed my people from slavery. You will call this celebration Passover." All the Israelites hurry to follow God's instructions. At midnight, God sends his death angel to kill the firstborn son of every Egyptian family—from the firstborn son of the prisoners in Egypt's dungeons to the firstborn son of Pharaoh himself.

Egypt is filled with the sound of crying. Pharaoh calls for Moses and Aaron one last time. "Go!" he shouts at them. "Free the slaves! Take your people and all your animals and get out of here!"

The Israelites quickly gather their children, animals, and belongings. They hurry out of Egypt as fast as they can go.

To learn more about the 10 plagues and the Israelites' deliverance from Egypt, read Exodus 5–12.

"Wow!" Lana says. "I've read about the 10 plagues so many times, but I've never realized how bad they really were. God's power is amazing!"

"I can't believe Pharaoh held out for so long," Griffin says, shaking his head. "I mean, why didn't he just listen to God?" The bus heads for the vast desert, following the long line of Israelites marching toward freedom.

Moses leads the Israelites through the desert for many long and difficult days. It is hot. They are tired and hungry. But God is watching over them. He guides them with a pillar of cloud during the day and a pillar of fire during the night.

One day, Pharaoh changes his mind yet again. "I want my slaves back!" he says. He sends his soldiers to capture the Israelites and return them to Egypt.

The Israelites are camped at the edge of the Red Sea when the Egyptians catch up to them. God's people have nowhere to run.

The Israelites are frightened, but Moses knows that God will help them. "Lift your walking stick above the sea," God tells Moses. Moses obeys, lifting his staff high into the air. The sea splits right down the middle. A dry road forms, and the Israelites cross safely, all the way to the other side.

When the Egyptian soldiers try to cross, the wheels of their chariots get stuck in the sand. Water crashes down on them. Huge waves knock over and destroy their chariots. All of the soldiers are swept away and drown. Safe on the other side of the sea, the Israelites sing a song of praise to God for helping them.

To learn more about the crossing of the Red Sea, read Exodus 13:17–15:21.

The Lord is my strength and my song; he has given me victory. This is my God, and I will praise him—my father's God, and I will exalt him!

Exodus 15:2

PARK HERE!

READ AND MEMORIZE THIS VERSE.

Rest Stops

God continues to help the Israelites as they travel through the desert. When they come to an oasis whose water is too bitter to drink, all the people moan and complain. God shows Moses how to make it good to drink.

But soon the people are complaining again. "We are so hungry!" they wail. "God must have brought us into the desert just to kill us."

"I will give the people all the food they can eat!" God tells Moses. "I will show them my glory." God sends huge flocks of quail into the Israelites' camp. The Israelites build a campfire and dine on meat. The next morning the people look out of their tents and see something unusual on the ground.

"What is it?" they ask.

Someone picks up a piece of the strange substance and cautiously takes a bite. "It's delicious! God has sent us bread from heaven!" The

people joyfully gather all the food they need. They call the heavenly bread manna. God sends the manna each morning of the Israelites' journey through the desert.

One day, the Israelites run out of water, and they start complaining again. They surround Moses and yell at him. "Give us water, NOW!" they shout.

"What should I do?" Moses cries out to God. "These people are going to hurt me soon!"

"Take your staff," God says, "the same staff that Aaron used when I turned the Nile into blood. Hit that rock near Mount Sinai."

Moses hits the rock, and water gushes out. All the people have plenty to drink.

To learn more about how God provided for his people in the desert, read Exodus 15:22–17:7.

Rules of the Road

Munch pulls another peanut-butter-and-jelly sandwich out of his back pocket and takes a giant bite. Lana looks at him and smiles. "What?" he says, shrugging. "Watching the Israelites made me hungry!" The bus continues its journey through the desert. Munch shares his sandwich with Lana while Griffin consults the map.

"Looks like we're headed back to Mount Sinai," Griffin says. As soon as he finishes speaking, there is a loud crack of thunder.

Thunder booms and lightning splits the sky. Moses and the Israelites are camping at the base of Mount Sinai. A thick cloud covers the mountain of God. The people have been getting ready for God to speak to them. A trumpet made from a ram's horn blows loud and long, and the people tremble with fear. The mountain smokes and shakes. Moses leads the people out of the camp to the foot of the mountain to meet with God. The people stare at the smoke and the lightning. They are terrified at this display of God's power.

God calls from the thunder for Moses to come up to him. Moses climbs to the top of the mountain to speak with God. He does not return for 40 days. "The Israelites need to understand that I am not like the fake gods they know," God says. "I am giving them a set of rules to live by."

Moses listens as God tells him about his rules. God even writes his laws on stone tablets with his own finger. "These are instructions on how to live in a way that pleases me," God says.

Down in the camp, the Israelites are getting impatient. "Where is Moses?" they shout. "He's supposed to be our leader, but he's abandoned us!" The Israelites grab Aaron. "You are his brother," they say to him. "Do something. Build us a god. We can't make it in this desert on our own."

Aaron fears the people will hurt him if he doesn't give them what they want. "All right," he says. "Everybody bring me a gold earring." Women, children, and men line up to place their gold jewelry in Aaron's hands. When the line ends, Aaron looks down at the earrings. The gold sparkles in the sunlight.

BUILD YOUR FAITH!

God gave Moses, the Israelites, and us a set of rules to live by. Those rules are called the Ten Commandments. You have many rules that you are expected to follow. Who sets rules for you? Do your parents set rules about your bedtime? Do your teachers set rules for the classroom? What are some of the laws our government makes? Why do we need traffic rules when driving a car or riding a bike? Rules are designed to help us live a good life and be safe. How does following God's rules help you in your life?

The Ten Commandments

When the Israelites were camped near Mount Sinai, God made a covenant, or agreement, with them. He promised to be with them, protecting them and giving them everything they needed. In return, the people were to live in a way that was pleasing to God. The Ten Commandments explain how to live in a way that honors God and makes him happy.

You must not have any other god but me.

You must not make for yourself an idol of any kind.

You must not misuse the name of the Lord your God.

Remember to observe the Sabbath day by keeping it holy.

Honor your father and mother.

You must not murder.

You must not commit adultery.

You must not steal.

You must not testify falsely against your neighbor.

You must not covet anything that belongs to your neighbor.

The Ten Commandments can be found in Exodus 20:1-21 and Deuteronomy 5:6-21.

Aaron takes the gold and melts it in a hot fire. Then he takes the melted gold and shapes it into a calf. The people are excited when they see the calf. It looks like one of the Egyptians' gods. "Now there's a real god!" they shout. "Good work, Aaron!"

Aaron builds an altar in front of the gold calf. "We'll have a big party tomorrow to worship our god!" he tells the people. They get up early the next morning and bring offerings to the calf. Some men play music while others dance. Women busy themselves preparing a feast for all.

God sees what his people are up to. "Go back down the mountain!" he tells Moses. "The people have already rejected me as their God! They have made themselves a fake god out of gold."

Moses returns down the side of the mountain with God's laws in his hands. He hears the sounds of the party. "What are you doing?" Moses shouts at the people. His face turns red with rage. "You are all sinners, worshiping a false god!" Moses is so angry that he smashes the stone tablets with God's laws against the ground. Then he destroys the gold calf.

"How could you allow this to happen?" he says to his brother.

"I was only doing what the people wanted," Aaron replies. "They thought you left them."

"You fool!" Moses says. "There is only one true God!" Moses goes back up on the mountain to ask God to forgive the people. God writes his laws on stone tablets again to replace the ones that Moses broke.

To learn more about God's laws, read Exodus 19–34.

Scouting Ahead

"Moses," God says, "I want you to send men out to explore Canaan—the land I am going to give to the Israelites. Send one man from each of the 12 tribes."

Moses chooses 12 men. One of them is his assistant Joshua. Joshua's friend Caleb also goes along. "Go and explore the land of Canaan," Moses tells them. "Tell us what it is like there. What are the people like? Is the land fertile or bad for growing crops? Are the cities well defended? What kind of food do they eat?"

The men agree and set out on their journey. When they return, the Israelites are excited to hear about the land God promised them. "Tell us about the land of Canaan," someone shouts.

"The land is rich and beautiful," one of the men says.

"The crops are delicious," another man says, showing the people some of the fruit they brought back. "It is good land." But most of the spies don't look happy. They are frowning and looking at the ground.

"So what's the problem?" someone asks.

"The Canaanites are very strong, and their cities are well protected. We could never conquer them!"

"We even saw giants there!" another man says. "We looked like grasshoppers next to them!"

The people begin to cry loudly. "God has led us all the way here only to have us die in battle!" they yell. "We should give up and go back to Egypt!"

"No, we shouldn't!" Caleb and Joshua interrupt, running out among the people. "Canaan is a beautiful land! So what if the Canaanites are huge and the cities have high walls? If God is pleased with us, he will help us. God will lead us into the land he has promised us. With God's help, we can conquer it!"

The other 10 spies ignore Caleb and Joshua and continue spreading doubt among the Israelites. "We could never win a battle in Canaan!" they say. Soon all of the Israelites are discouraged.

"Let's just go back to Egypt!" they shout.

God is furious that his people still don't trust him. "Because you are unfaithful to me, none of you who are 20 years old or older will see the land of Canaan," he tells them. "You have seen my glory. You have seen all I have done for you, both in Egypt and in the desert, but you still do not obey me. The only people over 20 years old who will enter the Promised Land are Caleb and Joshua. The rest of you will die in this desert. You and your children will wander in this desert for the next 40 years."

To learn more about the 12 spies, read Numbers 13–14.

A New Guide for Israel

The bus travels through the desert for a long, long time. The ride is uneventful, and Lana, Griffin, and Munch fall asleep in their seats.

Griffin is awakened by the sound of rushing water. "Look!" He shakes Lana and Munch by the shoulders. The three kids peer out the window at a sign that reads, "The Jordan River."

Joshua stands on the bank of the Jordan River and stares at its rising water. The river is in flood stage, and Joshua wonders how he and the Israelites will cross. Hearing sounds of laughter, he glances over his shoulder at the Israelites' camp. He smiles at the sight of their tents, clustered under the trees of Acacia Grove. Moses faithfully led the people for a long time. But now Moses is dead, and Joshua knows it is his turn to lead. Turning back to the river, Joshua loses his smile. "What if this job is too big for me?" he asks God.

"Be strong and courageous!" God tells him. "Don't be afraid. Obey all of the instructions Moses gave you, and I will be with you every step of the way."

To learn more about what God said to Joshua, read Joshua 1:1-9.

JORDAN RIVER

- The Jordan River is a shallow river located in western Asia. It flows to the Dead Sea.
- Ancient civilizations settled near rivers because water was a much-needed resource. Also, the river would flood, leaving behind rich soil for farming.
- The rivers of ancient civilizations were sometimes used for travel in order to trade goods. But the Jordan River was not used this way in biblical times. Instead, it served as a natural barrier or border for lands.
- The Jordan River was the site where John the Baptist baptized Jesus. It was also the river crossed when the Israelites entered the Promised Land.

Fun Fact: The Jordan River is mentioned in the Bible approximately 190 times!

This is my command—be strong and courageous! Do not be afraid or discouraged. For the LORD your God is with you wherever you go.

Joshua 1:9

PARK HERE!

READ AND MEMORIZE THIS VERSE.

A Secret Trip to Jericho

The sun is setting as the bus continues driving through the desert. Lana squints her eyes against the glare, trying to see out the window. Then suddenly something catches the light of the sinking sun. It's another sign. "Jericho!" she shouts, making Munch and Griffin jump. "We're driving right into the city!"

"It's true," Griffin says. "Look at that massive wall!" He cranes his neck as the bus drives through the city gates. A delicious aroma wafts through the windows of the bus.

Munch sniffs. "I smell food!"

The bus turns a corner onto a wide street. It stops in front of a house built right into the wall. The sound of talking and laughter spills out of the open door and windows. The kids have a clear view into the home. A beautiful woman moves around inside the house, serving food and drinks to her noisy guests.

"Look there!" Lana says suddenly, making the boys jump again.

"You've got to stop that, Lana," Munch grumbles.

"Shhh!" Lana points to two shadowy figures making their way quietly down the street. They sneak into the house and try to blend in among the guests.

"Those men don't belong there," Munch says.

"They must be Joshua's spies!" Lana says excitedly.

The woman approaches the two strangers who made their way into her home. “Hello, my name is Rahab,” she says. “Welcome to my house. May I get you a drink?”

“No, thank you,” one of the men says. “We are just traveling through and need a place to stay for the night.”

Rahab notices the man’s accent. *These men are not from Jericho,* she thinks. *They must be some of the Hebrews that everyone is talking about.*

“Well, you have come to the right place,” she says out loud. “You will be very comfortable here.” But the men don’t seem comfortable at all. They look around nervously and can’t stand still. “Is something wrong?” Rahab asks.

“Of course not,” the second man says. “We are just tired from our journey.” Rahab nods.

But the truth is the men are nervous. They are afraid that the other guests will recognize that they are Hebrews. Joshua has sent them to spy on Jericho. They have come to gather information about the city so that Joshua can use it to plan his attack.

One of the other guests overhears the conversation between Rahab and the two men. He sneaks out to warn the king that there are Hebrews in Jericho. Rahab sees him go. She knows that the two men could be in great danger.

JERICHO

- Jericho is a city located in the modern nation of Israel. Jericho is sometimes called the city of palm trees because a lot of palm trees grew there during biblical times. The city was built on top of a mound near the Jordan River.
- Jericho had rich soil that was good for growing crops. Natural springs were located in Jericho, making the city an oasis in the middle of the desert.
- In Joshua’s time, there was a defensive wall around the city of Jericho. Many of the houses were built right into the city wall.
- Houses in Jericho had flat roofs used for sleeping and storing food.

Fun Fact: Jericho is believed by some to be the oldest city in the world!

Rahab takes the Hebrews aside. "We must act quickly," she says. "The king will soon find out that you are in Jericho."

"What should we do?" one of the men asks Rahab.

"Come with me," she says. Rahab takes both men upstairs, to the roof of her home. "You will be safe up here," she says. The men lie down on the floor, and Rahab buries them under bundles of flax. Then she hurries back downstairs.

Rahab has hardly reached the bottom step when she hears pounding on the door. She takes a deep breath and answers it. Some of the king's men are standing outside.

"The king orders that you bring out the Hebrew spies who are staying here!" one of them shouts.

"The men you are looking for were here earlier," Rahab says. "But they left my home at dusk, just before the city gates closed. If you hurry, you might be able to catch them." The king's men rush away.

Later that night, Rahab goes back up to the roof to talk with the men. "The Lord, your God, is the supreme God of the heavens and the earth," she says. "I know he has given you this land. We are all afraid of the Israelites." She clasps her hands together in her lap. "I have risked everything to help you," she says. "I only ask for one thing in return."

"What is it?" the men ask.

"When you attack Jericho, spare my life and the lives of my family members," Rahab says.

The men nod. "If you don't tell anyone where to find us, we will personally guarantee your safety," they promise.

Rahab lowers the men down from one of her windows with a rope. "Go into the hills and hide for three days," she tells them. "Once the men who are looking for you come back to Jericho, you will be safe to travel again."

The men thank her. Before leaving, they tell Rahab to hang a scarlet rope from the window so that the Israelite soldiers know which home to pass over. "The night of the attack, bring all of your family members here inside this house," they tell her. "If they go out into the street and are killed, that will not be our fault. But as long as your relatives remain inside this house, they will be protected. We will not destroy this home."

Rahab agrees and sends the spies on their way. For three days, they hide in the hills; then they report back to Joshua.

To learn more about Rahab, read Joshua 2.

The bus heads back to the Jordan River, where the Israelites are packing up their camp. "It looks like everyone is leaving," Munch says.

"They are," Griffin replies. "They're headed to Jericho—but first they have to cross the Jordan River." Griffin and Munch stare at the raging water. It is higher than ever, pouring over the sides of the embankment and splashing at Joshua's feet.

"The priests will cross first, with the Ark of the Covenant," Joshua tells his people. He points at the beautifully decorated box topped by two winged angels made out of gold. Four priests, dressed in white, respectfully approach the Ark. Leaning down, they pick up the poles used to carry the Ark and lift them to their shoulders. "Follow the priests across the river, but make sure to stay a good distance away from the Ark," the leaders tell the people.

The Israelites understand that the Ark is holy and to be revered. It symbolizes the throne of God. Inside the Ark are the stone tablets with the Ten Commandments, a jar of manna, and the staff of Aaron, the first high priest, who died in the wilderness.

At Joshua's command, the priests start walking toward the flooding river. They go forward without stopping, stepping right into the water. When the priests walk into the river, the water stops flowing. The people gasp as they watch a dry, rocky path form through the middle of the river. "Come on, let's cross," Joshua says. He motions for the Israelites to follow. When the priests reach the middle of the riverbed, they stop and wait for everyone to cross to the other side.

Safe on the opposite shore, Joshua kneels and thanks God. God delivers this message to Joshua: "Pick 12 men from among the people, one from each tribe. Tell each man to choose a large stone from the middle of the river. They should place the stones in a pile where you camp tonight."

Joshua obeys. He chooses 12 men and sends them back to the riverbed. "Fetch the largest stone you can find," he tells them. Each of the 12 men carries a giant stone all the way to the new campsite. That night, the men build a memorial using the stones. Placing his hand on top of the stone monument, Joshua says, "May we always remember the miracle that took place today at the Jordan River."

To learn more about the crossing of the Jordan River, read Joshua 3–4.

Going in Circles

The bus follows the Israelite army as they march toward Jericho. Munch presses his nose against the bus window as the city comes into view. "I know which Bible story is next," he whispers. Turning to his friends, he says, "We are about to see the entire wall of Jericho come crashing to the ground!"

The city gates of Jericho are shut tight. Nobody is going in or coming out. *How will we ever capture this city if we can't get inside?* Joshua wonders. Joshua knows the Israelites must conquer Jericho before they can live in the Promised Land, but he also knows there is no way they can win this battle without God on their side. Joshua walks around the city, looking up at the huge wall. He prays for God's help.

As he rounds the corner, Joshua sees a man holding a sword in his hand! Remembering that God told him to be brave, Joshua marches right up to the man. "Hey!" he says. "Are you a friend or an enemy?"

"Neither," the man replies. "I am the commander of God's army."

Realizing this is an answer to his prayers, Joshua falls to the ground. "I will do whatever you tell me," he says. "What are your instructions?"

"Take off your sandals," the commander tells Joshua. "This is a holy place." Joshua immediately obeys, removing his shoes and setting them aside. The commander continues, "Here is what you must do to conquer Jericho. March with your soldiers around the city wall once a day for six days. The priests must

BUILD YOUR FAITH!

God's strategy for conquering Jericho didn't make much sense to Joshua, but he obeyed God's instructions anyway. Have your parents or a teacher ever told you to do something that didn't make sense to you? Did you obey them anyway? How did the situation turn out? You need to trust that your parents know what's best for you and follow their instructions even when you don't understand why. In the same way, God asks his people to trust him and do what he says even when his instructions don't seem to make sense.

The Promised Land

The people of Israel were divided into twelve tribes, or family groups. Each tribe was named after one of Jacob's sons (Joseph's tribe was split into two groups, Ephraim and Manasseh, named after Joseph's two sons). When the Israelites entered the Promised Land, Joshua gave each tribe their own territory in which to live—except for the tribe of Levi. Because the Levites were the priests, they were given towns in the other tribes' lands so that every tribe would have priests living near them.

NAPHTALI
Kedesh
ASHER
ZEBULUN
ISSACHAR
Golan
Ramoth-gilead
Shechem
JOSEPH
GAD

To learn more about the twelve tribes of Israel and their land, read Genesis 49:1-28; Joshua 13:1–21:45.

go with you, carrying the Ark of the Covenant and blowing their trumpets. But the soldiers must be completely silent—they should not shout any battle cries or talk at all. Then, on the seventh day, march around the city wall seven times, and when the priests blow their trumpets, have everyone shout as loud as they can. Then the wall will crumble to the ground."

Joshua has never heard of anyone winning a battle just by playing trumpets and shouting, but he trusts God and does as he is told. He orders his soldiers to march around the wall without saying a word.

THINK ABOUT IT!

[God said to Joshua,] "Be sure to give this land to Israel as a special possession, just as I have commanded you."
Joshua 13:6

Joshua assigned each Israelite tribe its own territory, except the Levites, who lived in special towns scattered throughout the entire land. God gave the Levites the job of serving as spiritual leaders to the entire nation. Two and a half tribes—Reuben, Gad, and half the tribe of Manasseh—got land on the east side of the Jordan River. The other half of the tribe of Manasseh lived across the Jordan from their relatives.

They do this every day for six days, while puzzled Jericho soldiers watch from the top of the wall and make fun of them.

On the seventh day, the Israelite army marches around the city seven times. Finally, the priests blast their trumpets long and loud. "Shout as loud as you can!" Joshua yells to his men. "God has given us this city!"

When the soldiers shout, the wall of Jericho shakes. Huge stones break apart and crash to the ground. In a matter of minutes, the entire wall collapses. The Israelites charge through huge clouds of dust and take control of the city. “Hooray!” they shout. “God helped us conquer Jericho!”

Joshua looks around at the destruction. One part of the wall still stands—the section that contains Rahab’s house. Her home has been completely spared. Joshua stares in wonder. Then he races to find the two spies he sent to Rahab’s house earlier. “Find Rahab,” he tells them. “Keep your promise to her and bring her and her family out of the city. They will be part of our people now.”

To learn more about the fall of Jericho, read Joshua 5:13–6:27.

Deborah in the Driver's Seat

"Spinning sprockets! That was amazing!" Munch says as the bus pulls away from Jericho.

"So what now?" Griffin asks. "Do the Israelites move into the Promised Land?"

"I bet they live happily ever after," Munch adds.

"Not exactly," Lana says, turning pages in the Bible. "The Israelites do settle in the Promised Land, but they don't completely drive out the people who were living there. They let some of them stay. Pretty soon, the Israelites start worshiping fake gods, and the true God allows their enemies to rule over them."

"Aw, man!" Munch says.

"But God still cares about them," Lana says. "He sends people called judges to help them out."

A large palm tree comes into view through the bus window. Griffin recognizes the landmark on the map. "That tree must be the Palm of Deborah," he says.

"Deborah was one of God's judges!" Lana exclaims.

Deborah sits in her favorite spot, under the shade of a giant palm tree. She is waiting for a man named Barak. Every few minutes, an Israelite approaches, asking for her help. The people know God is with Deborah, and so they come to seek advice and settle disagreements. Deborah doesn't mind. She gives Israelite after Israelite advice, while keeping an eye out for Barak.

The Israelites are suffering under the cruel reign of Jabin, a Canaanite king, and his army commander, Sisera. Just the mention of Sisera's name makes even the bravest Israelite soldier shake with fear. God has given Deborah a special message. "It is time for King Jabin's rule over my people to end," God told her. "Send for Barak, son of Abinoam, from the tribe of Naphtali. He will lead my people to victory over Sisera."

In the distance, Deborah spies a skinny man walking slowly toward her. *Could that be Barak?* she wonders. *That man doesn't look like a mighty warrior or great general.* The man makes his way over to where Deborah is sitting. He says, "I am Barak. You wanted to see me?"

Deborah looks Barak over. She isn't impressed, but she trusts that God knows what he is doing. "Thank you for coming, Barak," she says. "I have a message from God for you. God wants you to call 10,000 warriors from the tribes of Naphtali and Zebulun and go fight Sisera. He will give you victory."

Barak knows that Sisera has a huge army and 900 chariots. He isn't sure that he can win.

"I'll fight Sisera if you'll come with me," he tells Deborah.

Deborah stares at Barak. He shifts uncomfortably. "Fine," she says at last. "I will go with you. But a woman will get the honor for this victory against Sisera."

Barak gathers his troops, and he, Deborah, and the soldiers go to the top of Mount Tabor to prepare for battle. When Sisera hears that Israel has formed an army, he laughs. "We will crush them," he says. He summons his army and leads them to attack the Israelites.

Barak and his soldiers see Sisera's army coming. They rush down the slopes of the mountain, trying to catch the men off guard. God fights for Israel by pouring rain down from the sky. The ground becomes a muddy mess, making it impossible for the Canaanite soldiers to drive their chariots.

Sisera soon realizes that he has lost the battle. His chariot wheels are stuck tight in the mud, so he jumps down and runs away from the battlefield on foot.

Sisera runs until he is almost too tired to take another step. Finally, he sees a tent in the distance. "I'm saved!" he gasps. He knows that the tent belongs to a man named Heber, who is a friend of King Jabin.

Heber's wife, Jael, watches Sisera come toward her tent. She knows that he is the army commander of her husband's friend, the king. But Jael is following the instructions of a greater King than Jabin.

Jael goes out to meet Sisera. "Come into the tent, sir," she says. "Don't be afraid." Sisera collapses on the floor of the tent, and Jael covers him with a blanket.

"Water, please," Sisera croaks. Jael gives him milk to drink instead. "Stand at the door of your tent," Sisera orders her. "If anybody comes, tell them I'm not here." Soon, Sisera is fast asleep.

Jael knows what she must do. Quickly and quietly, she kills Sisera. Then she waits.

Before long, Barak comes looking for Sisera. Jael goes outside to meet him. "Come with me," she says. "I'll show you the man you're looking for."

Barak follows Jael into the tent. His mouth drops open with shock when he sees Sisera lying on the ground, dead. He stares at Jael. "You did this?" he says. Jael nods. "Deborah was right," Barak says. "The honor for the victory against Sisera belongs to a woman."

To learn more about Deborah, read Judges 4–5.

A Reluctant Leader

Rustling and banging sounds come from a pit in the ground. The pit is normally used to make grapes into wine, but today a man is hiding there. His name is Gideon, and he's hiding from his enemies, the Midianites. The Midianites are thieves who ride across the Israelites' land stealing their food and farm animals. The Israelites are hungry, and there is no food to spare. That is why Gideon is working in secret. He has worked underground all day threshing wheat. "The Midianites will never find this grain," he mutters as he beats the grain with a stick—*thwack, thwack, thwack*.

Gideon's back hurts, and his arms are sore. Needing a break, he climbs out of the pit and looks around to make sure his hiding place has not been revealed. Looking over his shoulder, he sees someone sitting beneath a huge tree. Gideon trips, nearly falling back down into the hole. "Who . . . who are you?" he stammers.

"Gideon," the stranger says, "you are a hero! God is with you!"

"I'm pretty sure you're mistaken," Gideon says. "I'm no hero—I'm just a nobody from a small clan of the tribe of Manasseh. And if God is with us, why are the Midianites causing us so much trouble? It looks to me like God has abandoned us."

"Gideon," the stranger says, "you can save your country from the Midianites! I will be with you and help you win the battle against them."

Gideon is doubtful. "I'm going to need some proof that you're really giving me a message from God," he says. "Please stay here while I get an offering."

"Go ahead," the stranger says. "I'll wait right here until you get back."

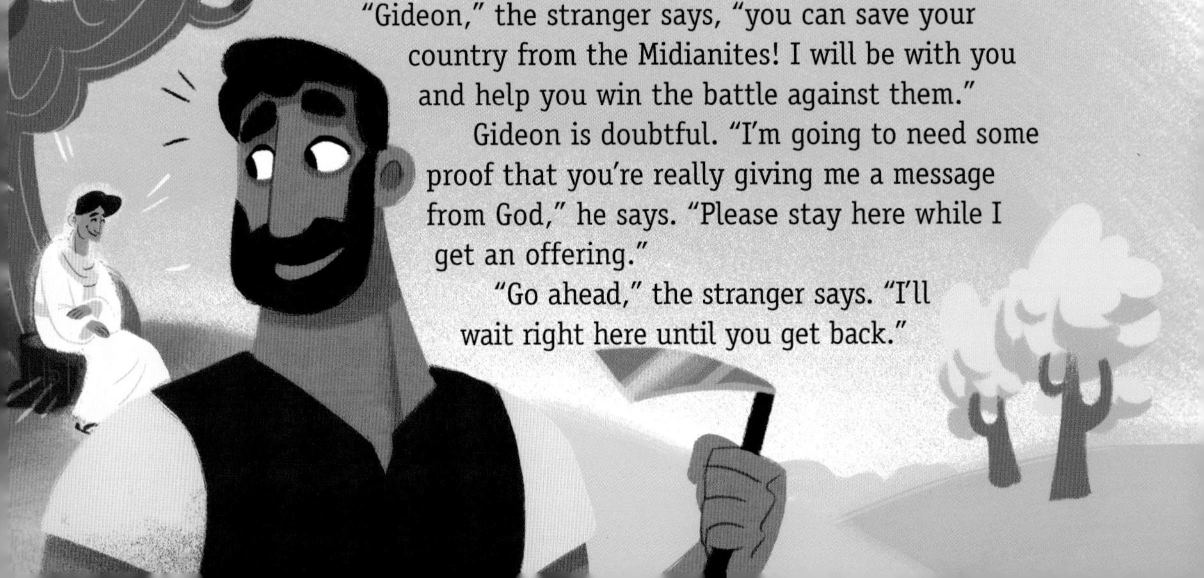

When Gideon returns with his offering, the stranger tells him to place it on a large rock. Then the stranger touches the offering with his staff. The offering bursts into flames, and the stranger disappears!

"Oh!" Gideon shouts. "That was the angel of the Lord! I saw him face-to-face—I'm doomed!" But God tells Gideon not to be afraid.

Gideon starts calling warriors from different tribes of Israel to fight against the Midianites. But once his soldiers have gathered, Gideon starts to get nervous.

"Lord, give me a sign," Gideon says. "I will place a wool fleece on the ground tonight. When I wake up, if the wool is wet with dew but the ground is dry, then I will know you are really telling me what to do."

The next morning, Gideon rushes to check the wool. Sure enough, the wool is wet and the ground is dry. Gideon picks up the wool and wrings a whole bowlful of water out of it. But Gideon is still not convinced. He wants another sign from God.

"I will put the wool out again tonight," Gideon tells God. "Tomorrow morning, if the wool is dry and the ground is wet, then I will know you are really speaking to me."

THINK ABOUT IT!

Gideon son of Joash was threshing wheat at the bottom of a winepress to hide the grain from the Midianites.

Judges 6:11

Gideon was preparing his wheat to be ground into flour through a process called *threshing*. Farmers would beat the wheat with a stick or a paddle to separate the edible inner part of the grains from the outer shell, called chaff. After beating the grain, the farmer would toss it into the air. Grain was normally threshed in a large, open area so that the wind could carry away the chaff. Threshing wheat in a pit, like Gideon was doing, would have been difficult, frustrating work.

SLOW!

The next morning, Gideon goes to check his fleece again. He finds that the wool is completely dry and the ground is soaked. "I'm convinced," Gideon says. "I will do whatever you ask."

"You have too many warriors," God tells Gideon. "I want everyone to know that you are going to win this battle only because I'm helping you." Gideon tells all the soldiers that they can go home if they're afraid. Lots of warriors leave, but God tells Gideon that he still has too many.

"Take your army to get a drink of water from this spring," God says. "I'll show you which soldiers to keep."

At the stream, Gideon watches as some of the men kneel down on the ground and put their mouths right in the water to drink. Others make a cup with their hands. God tells Gideon to take the men who cup water in their hands to fight the Midianites. It's a tiny army of only 300 men. *How will we win with such a small army?* Gideon wonders.

Under the cover of darkness, the Israelite soldiers prepare for battle against the Midianites. Gideon hands each man a trumpet, a clay jar, and a torch. He tells them what they are supposed to do with these strange weapons. They creep toward the campsite of their enemies and wait for Gideon's signal. When Gideon gives the sign, each man blows his trumpet, breaks his jar, and holds his torch high. "A sword for the Lord and for Gideon!" they yell.

The sudden noises and lights make the Midianites panic. They dash around the camp, swinging their swords wildly. They end up fighting each other. Those who are not killed run far away into the darkness. The Midianites never recover from this defeat. God has saved his people again.

To learn more about Gideon, read Judges 6–7.

Strong Man, Weak Leader

Lana watches out the window as the bus drives past field after field of grain. The sun shines down from a cloudless sky, making the grain shimmer like gold. Catching a glimpse of a woman in one field, Lana sits a little higher in her seat to get a better look. The woman sits alone in the middle of the grain. In the distance, others are busily working the field. At first Lana thinks maybe the woman is just resting and enjoying the weather. But as she looks closer, Lana realizes the woman is crying. Lana motions for Griffin and Munch to look. The three kids stare sadly at the woman, wishing they could help.

"Who is she?" Munch asks.

"I'm not sure," Lana says, reaching for the Bible.

The woman in the field sighs. Every time she hears the laughter of a child helping his or her parents in the nearby field, she cannot hold back the tears. The woman and her husband, Manoah, don't have any children. But she wishes they did.

These are difficult days not only for Manoah and his wife, but also for the whole nation of Israel. Once again, they have disobeyed God, and he has allowed a people called the Philistines to rule over them.

The woman closes her eyes and takes a deep breath, preparing herself to get back to work. But when she opens her eyes, she gets the surprise of a lifetime. There is an angel standing next to her, shining with glory! The woman is speechless. She doesn't move a muscle.

The angel speaks. "You are going to have a son," the angel says. "He will be special, set apart for God from the moment of his birth until the moment of his death."

"A son?" the woman whispers.

The angel continues, "You must not drink wine or other alcohol, or eat grapes or raisins. And your child's hair must never be cut. One day, he will rescue the Israelites from the Philistines."

"My son will be a hero?" the woman whispers again. When the angel disappears, the woman abandons her work and rushes to find her husband.

Some time later, Manoah's wife gives birth to a baby boy, and she names him Samson. She follows all of the angel's instructions. She never cuts Samson's hair.

Samson grows—and his hair grows—and his strength grows. Soon it becomes clear that Samson is much stronger than any other man. "His power can only come from God," Manoah says to his wife.

Samson's parents love having such a strong son to help them out around the house. Samson makes them very proud—until the day he comes home and says, "I want to marry a Philistine girl!" His parents are devastated.

"Why?" they ask him. "There are so many nice Israelite girls who would love to marry you. And you know that the Philistines worship false gods."

But Samson is just as stubborn as he is strong. "I love this girl. I'm going to marry her," he says.

And he does. The Philistines don't like the marriage any more than the Israelites do. They play a trick on Samson. He gets so angry that he kills 30 Philistines. In revenge, the Philistines kill Samson's wife. So Samson kills even more Philistines. Then the Philistines start attacking the Israelites.

Samson fights the Philistines for many years. The Philistines try everything they can think of to get rid of Samson, but he is too strong. "Where does he get such strength?" they wonder.

Soon, Samson falls in love with another Philistine woman. Her name is Delilah, and though she loves Samson, she loves money even more. The Philistines offer her a lot of money to figure out how Samson can be beaten. "We'll give you all of this," they say, showing her a chest full of silver coins.

Delilah runs her fingers over the shiny silver. "Leave it to me," she says. "I'll figure out Samson's secret."

Delilah gives Samson a fake smile. "Tell me the secret of your strength," she says sweetly.

Samson teases Delilah by telling her a lie. "Tie me up with seven new bowstrings, and I'll be just like anyone else."

Delilah ties Samson with the bowstrings and calls the Philistines to come get him. But Samson breaks free easily.

Delilah tries again, and Samson lies to her twice more. "Why won't you tell me the truth?" Delilah pouts. "You must not really love me." She begs Samson for days. Finally, he gives in.

"All right!" he shouts. "I'll tell you! My hair has never been cut. If my head were shaved, my special strength would leave me, and I would be as weak as anyone else."

"Samson has finally told me his real secret," Delilah reports to the Philistines. "This time, you'll be able to capture him." The Philistines hide outside Delilah's room as she soothes Samson to sleep with his head in her lap. Once he is asleep, she calls someone to shave his head. Then the Philistines burst in and take Samson prisoner. Samson tries to break free, but his power is gone!

The Philistines blind Samson and throw him in a dungeon. They tie him up with chains and force him to grind grain. But soon his hair starts to grow back.

One day, the Philistines throw a huge party to worship their fake god Dagon. "Dagon helped us defeat Samson," they cheer. The people dance and eat and drink until they can hardly stand. "Let's bring out Samson so we can make fun of him!" the people shout.

A young servant leads Samson out of the prison to Dagon's temple. "Put my hands on the pillars so I can lean against them," Samson says. Once he is standing between the pillars, Samson prays a final time. "God, please let me have one last victory over the Philistines."

God gives Samson strength once more. With a mighty heave, Samson knocks over the pillars he is leaning on and collapses the temple. Thousands of people die, including Samson. His last victory over the Philistines is his biggest.

To learn more about Samson, read Judges 13–16.

A Side Trip to Moab

The bus pulls away from the wreckage of Dagon's temple and onto the road. Suddenly, the engine revs up, and the bus zooms forward. "Whoooooaaaa!" Lana, Munch, and Griffin are thrown backward against their seats.

Munch struggles to sit up. "Aw, man!" he says. One of his pants pockets is purple and sticky. "My sandwich got squished." Lana grimaces as she looks at his pocket.

"Do you see the map?" Griffin asks, looking around. "It flew out of my hands." The three kids search between seats and on the floor.

"Found it!" Lana says, waving it around in the air. Griffin races to get the map. Opening it, he says, "Next stop: Moab."

Three women stand at a crossroads in Moab. They cry and hug each other. One of the women is older than the others. Her face is tired and sad.

The woman's name is Naomi. She is from a town in Israel called Bethlehem, but many years ago, she moved to Moab with her husband,

Elimelech, and their two sons, Mahlon and Kilion. There was no rain in Bethlehem for a very long time, making it difficult to grow crops. Food was running out, so Elimelech decided to take his wife and their sons to Moab. The family was happy there, and in time the two sons married Moabite women, Orpah and Ruth.

But then terrible things started to happen. Elimelech died, and about 10 years later so did both of the sons. Naomi and her two daughters-in-law were left sad and alone.

Naomi was heartbroken. She missed her husband, her sons, and her home. "I am going to move back to Bethlehem," she told Orpah and Ruth. "Moab doesn't feel like home anymore."

"We will come with you," the young women said. At first Naomi agreed, and they packed up all of their belongings and set out on the journey back to Bethlehem.

But now, partway into the trip, Naomi has had a change of heart. She turns to her daughters-in-law and says, "You both should return to Moab. You are young and have your whole lives ahead of you. You still have the opportunity to marry again and have children. I cannot have more sons. There is no future for you with me."

MOAB

- Moab is located in modern-day Jordan. It was built on a plateau of a mountainous region, which also included pastures.
- The land of Moab was named after Moab, the son of Lot.
- Moab received plenty of rainfall, especially in the winter. Lots of settlements have been found near Moab, suggesting the land was good for growing crops.
- Moab was located along a trading route. Moab had desirable natural resources such as limestone (for building), salt (for cooking and preserving food), and balsam (for making medicine).

Fun Fact: In 1868, a German missionary, F. A. Klein, found a large black basalt stone with an inscription on it near the ruins of Dibon. It came to be called "The Moabite Stone." The inscription contained a record of the wars of Mesha, the king of Moab. Many of the names on the stone also appear in the Bible.

The women weep together. Orpah kisses Naomi good-bye and turns back toward her homeland. But Ruth says, "Don't ask me to leave you and return to Moab. Wherever you go, I will go; wherever you live, I will live. Wherever you die, I will die." Naomi cannot convince Ruth to return to Moab. So Ruth and Naomi set out to make a new life for themselves in Bethlehem.

"Guess we're headed to Bethlehem with Naomi and Ruth," Munch says, as the bus continues on.

"Yep," Lana agrees. "I'm really happy that Ruth chose to stay by Naomi's side."

When they arrive in Bethlehem, Ruth goes to collect grain in a field. She walks behind the men who are harvesting the grain, picking up what they drop. She works as hard as she can to gather grain so that she and Naomi will have something to eat. The field belongs to a wealthy man named Boaz. He is a relative of Naomi's husband, Elimelech.

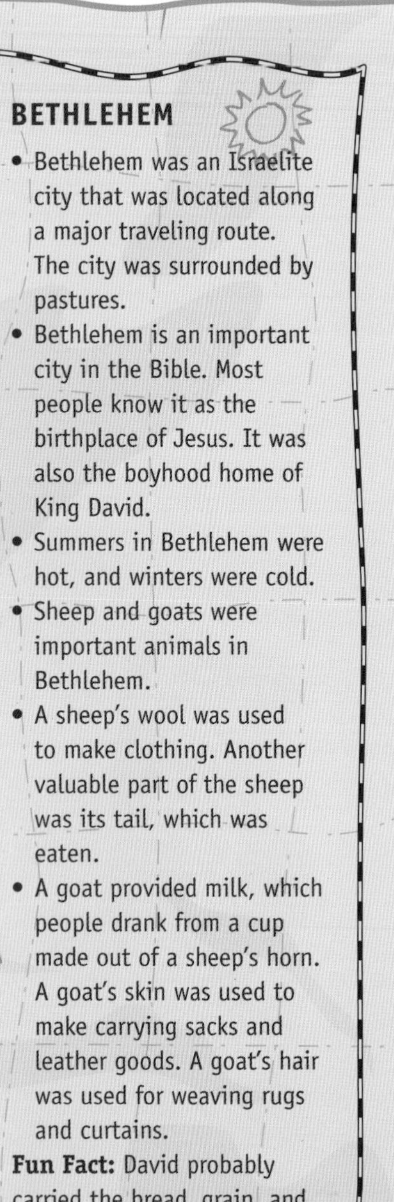

BETHLEHEM

- Bethlehem was an Israelite city that was located along a major traveling route. The city was surrounded by pastures.
- Bethlehem is an important city in the Bible. Most people know it as the birthplace of Jesus. It was also the boyhood home of King David.
- Summers in Bethlehem were hot, and winters were cold.
- Sheep and goats were important animals in Bethlehem.
- A sheep's wool was used to make clothing. Another valuable part of the sheep was its tail, which was eaten.
- A goat provided milk, which people drank from a cup made out of a sheep's horn. A goat's skin was used to make carrying sacks and leather goods. A goat's hair was used for weaving rugs and curtains.

Fun Fact: David probably carried the bread, grain, and cheese to his brothers at war using a sack made out of goatskin.

Boaz likes what he hears about Ruth and her faithfulness to Naomi. He makes sure that she gets plenty of grain to take home.

When Ruth gets home that night and shows her mother-in-law all the grain she gathered, Naomi can't believe her eyes! "Where did you get all this?" she asks.

"I worked in the field of a man named Boaz," Ruth replies. "He was very kind to me."

"May God bless him!" Naomi says. "He is one of our relatives." Naomi is quiet for a moment. "I wonder . . ." she says to herself.

Ruth works in Boaz's field for many weeks. One day, Naomi says to her, "It's time to find a new husband for you. Boaz is a good man. He is also one of our family redeemers, who can help us by marrying you and buying Elimelech's land that I need to sell. Tonight, he will be at the threshing floor. Go and meet with Boaz and ask him to be your family redeemer."

Ruth does everything that Naomi tells her to do. She takes a bath and puts on her nicest clothes. She even dabs on some perfume. Then she goes to the threshing floor to talk to Boaz. Following Naomi's instructions, Ruth waits until Boaz and his workers have all gone to sleep. Then she walks quietly over to Boaz. When he wakes up, Ruth asks him to marry her and buy Elimelech's land.

"Of course I want to marry you," Boaz says. "Everyone knows that you are good and kind." Ruth blushes. "But there is another man that is more closely related to your family than I am," Boaz continues. "I have to meet with this other man first. It is only right. But if he refuses to redeem you, then I will marry you myself!"

While it is still dark, Ruth goes home and tells Naomi everything that happened. "Don't worry, my daughter," Naomi says. "Boaz will settle everything."

Boaz meets with the other family redeemer. They agree that Boaz should be the one to marry Ruth.

Ruth and Naomi are overjoyed to hear the good news. "God has rewarded you for being so faithful to me," Naomi says, wiping away tears of joy.

Ruth and Boaz are soon married, and some time after that, they have a baby. They name him Obed. "I get to be a grandma now," Naomi says. She holds Obed close and thanks God for giving her a new family.

To learn more about Naomi and Ruth, read the book of Ruth.

The End of the Road for Israel's Judges

"That baby is the cutest!" Lana squeals.

Griffin hands Lana the Bible. "We're headed to Shiloh next," he says. "I'm anxious to hear who we are going to see."

Lana flips through the pages. "I'll give you a hint," she says. "We're going to see another cute baby! And this baby will grow up and deliver messages for the Lord."

The bus pulls up close to a huge tent made from animal skins. "That's the Tabernacle," Lana says. "It's a special tent where the Israelites go to worship God, kind of like how we go to church."

A woman named Hannah kneels in prayer at the Tabernacle in Shiloh. Folding her hands, she cries, "Lord, see my suffering. I desperately want a child of my own. Please give me a son to love. If you give me a son, I will dedicate his entire life to you. My son will serve you forever."

Eli, the priest, watches while the woman prays. He sees her mouth moving and her forehead wrinkle while tears run down her face, but he doesn't hear her saying anything. Eli thinks that Hannah is behaving badly because she has drunk too much wine. He goes over and scolds her for acting this way in God's house.

"I haven't had too much to drink," Hannah explains. "I'm just praying and pouring my heart out to the Lord. I'm very sad, and I am asking God to give me a son."

"In that case, go in peace, and I hope God answers your prayers," Eli says.

God does answer Hannah's prayers. About a year later, she gives birth to a baby boy and names him Samuel. Hannah and her husband, Elkanah, are so happy! But Hannah doesn't forget her promise to God.

When Samuel has grown from a baby into a little boy, Hannah and Elkanah take him to the Tabernacle. There, Hannah sees the high priest, Eli. "Sir, do you remember me?" she asks him. "A few years ago, I was here praying in anguish for God to give me a child."

"Yes, I remember," Eli says, looking down at the little boy holding his mother's hand. "I see God answered your prayers."

"He did," Hannah says, "and so I am here to keep my promise to him." Hannah brings Samuel to stand in front of her. "I am giving my son to the Lord," Hannah says. "I want Samuel to stay here with you and serve God his entire life." She nudges Samuel gently toward Eli.

SHILOH

- Shiloh was an ancient city located in the Ephraim hill country. It was the capital of Israel before the first Temple was built in Jerusalem.
- Shiloh served as a major religious center, and many people gathered to worship there. Because Shiloh was a pilgrimage site, people would have traveled to the city three times a year.
- When the Israelites settled in the Promised Land, the Tabernacle was set up permanently in Shiloh.
- The houses in Shiloh were made of mud brick with a stone foundation. They consisted of three or four rooms with a flat roof.
- A wall was built around the city of Shiloh for protection, and city gates led into the city.

Fun Fact: Archaeological evidence has been uncovered suggesting that at some point in biblical history, the city of Shiloh burned to the ground.

Eli reaches out and takes Samuel's hand. Eli has two sons of his own. Eli's sons are making bad choices, and he is disappointed in them.

Eli, Hannah, and Elkanah worship God together. Then, Elkanah and Hannah go home, leaving Samuel with Eli. Samuel learns how to help Eli in the Tabernacle.

One night when Samuel is still a boy, something amazing happens. It starts like any other night. Samuel says a bedtime prayer, pulls up his blankets, and falls asleep right away. But in the middle of the night, someone calls out his name. "Samuel!" the voice says.

"That must be Eli. I will go and see what he wants," says Samuel, climbing out of bed.

But Eli says that he didn't call. "Go back to sleep," he tells Samuel.

Samuel goes back to sleep. Then it happens again. "Samuel!"

Samuel gets out of bed again and runs to Eli. "I did not call you, my son. You must be dreaming. Go back to bed," Eli says.

Samuel goes back to bed. But then the voice calls a third time. Samuel goes to Eli again. "Here I am! Did you call me?"

This time, Eli wakes up completely. "Maybe it is God who is calling you," he says. "Next time you hear the voice, tell God you are listening."

Samuel goes back to bed. But now he cannot sleep. *What would God want with me?* Samuel wonders. He stares at the ceiling for a long time. Just as he is dozing off, he hears the voice again. "Samuel! Samuel!" the voice says.

"I'm listening, God," Samuel answers. "What do you want me to do?" God gives Samuel an important message. God tells Samuel that he is going to punish Eli's sons for all the terrible things they have done. And God is going to punish Eli for not stopping them.

The next morning, Samuel stays in bed as long as he can. He doesn't want to tell Eli about God's message. But as soon as Eli sees Samuel, Eli asks, "Was it God who was calling you last night? Did he have a message for you? Tell me everything." So Samuel tells Eli about his conversation with God. Eli is quiet for a long time. Then he sighs and puts his hand on Samuel's shoulder. "Let God do what he thinks is best," Eli says. From that point on, the Lord continues to visit Samuel. He makes Samuel his prophet, and Samuel delivers God's messages all over Israel.

To learn more about Samuel, read 1 Samuel 1–3.

The bus starts up, and Griffin checks the map. "Looks like we're heading toward a town called Ramah," he says.

A herd of donkeys crosses the road. "Look out!" Lana shouts. The bus swerves, nearly hitting them. The donkeys bray and start running. Soon, they've disappeared over the horizon.

The bus continues down the road a ways and stops. Two young men appear, covered in dust and looking tired.

"Have you seen any donkeys come through?" one of the young men asks an older man who is walking along the road. He shakes his head. The other young man speaks to a child who is climbing on a fence near the road. "How about you? Have you seen any donkeys?"

"No," the child says.

One of the men is named Saul, and the other is his servant. They have been traveling for days, searching all over for Saul's father's missing donkeys. They cannot find the donkeys anywhere.

Saul kicks a clump of grass. "Where did those donkeys get to?" he asks. "Let's just go home," he says to his servant. "By now my father will be more worried about us than about the donkeys."

"Wait! I just got an idea!" the servant says. "Maybe we should ask the prophet who lives in this town. Everything that he predicts comes true."

Saul agrees, and the two young men head into Ramah to find Samuel.

Along the way, they pass some young women coming to draw water at a well. "Is Samuel around today?" the young men ask.

"Yes," the women say. "He's at the town gates. If you hurry, you can catch up to him before he goes to the place of worship." Saul and his servant meet up with Samuel near the town gates.

Samuel is expecting Saul. He got a message from God about him the day before. "I am sending a man named Saul to you," the Lord had told Samuel. "Anoint him to be the leader of my people."

"Come to the place of worship with me," Samuel says to Saul.

"Let's get something to eat, and in the morning, I will tell you what you want to know. Don't worry about your donkeys. They have been found."

Saul is glad to hear about the donkeys, but he wonders what else Samuel might have to tell him. As the men walk toward the place of worship, Samuel turns to Saul and says, "You and your family are the hope of Israel."

Saul stares at Samuel. "I'm not anybody special," he says. "I come from the least important family of the smallest tribe in Israel! Why would you say that to me?"

When the men reach the place of worship, Saul notices a banquet has been prepared. His stomach rumbles as he looks around at the delicious food. "Come, sit here," Samuel says, seating Saul at the head of the table. Then he gives Saul the finest food at the banquet. *Why the special treatment?* Saul wonders. After the banquet, Samuel invites Saul and the servant to sleep at his house for the night.

Samuel wakes Saul early the next morning. "Time for you to go!" he says. "But first, I have an important message for you from God."

"What is it?" Saul asks.

Samuel takes a small bottle of oil and pours it over Saul's head. It feels smooth and slippery as it runs down Saul's neck. The spicy scent of the oil fills the air. "God has chosen you to become king of Israel," Samuel says. "You will lead God's people."

Some time later, Samuel calls the people of Israel together for a meeting. "God is going to give you the king you asked for," he tells them. "The new king is Saul!" Everyone looks around, anxious to get a glimpse of Israel's first king. But they can't find Saul anywhere.

Saul is too nervous to stand before the crowd as the king of Israel. He hides behind some baggage, where no one can see him.

The people ask God where their king is. "He's hiding behind the luggage," the Lord replies. A few men run to bring Saul out. They bring him over to Samuel. The people admire how tall the king is.

"This is the king God has chosen for you," Samuel declares.

"Long live the king!" the people shout. "Long live King Saul!"

To learn more about King Saul,
read 1 Samuel 9–10.

The bus pulls a U-turn and heads back down the road. An elderly man appears in the distance.

"Is that . . . yes, it's Samuel!" Lana says.

Samuel walks straight down the road. His head is bowed, and his shoulders are slumped. "What's wrong with Samuel?" Lana asks. "He looks so sad."

"And older, too," Munch adds. "His hair is a lot grayer than before."

"It looks like he is headed back to Bethlehem," Griffin says, consulting the map. "I wonder why."

Samuel is going to Bethlehem under orders from God. God wants Samuel to find a new king to replace Saul. King Saul started his reign well, but as time has passed, he has become proud and stubborn. He has started disobeying God. This makes Samuel very sad. He has tried many times to talk with Saul and point him in the right direction. But Saul will not listen. "It's time for a new king," God tells Samuel. "Go to Bethlehem and find a man named Jesse. One of his sons will be my new king."

Samuel meets Jesse and seven of Jesse's sons. "Come, join me in making a sacrifice," Samuel says to them. Jesse and his sons accept Samuel's invitation.

Samuel looks at the seven handsome young men standing before him. *Any one of these men would make a magnificent king,* he thinks.

Jesse introduces Samuel to his oldest son, Eliab. *This one is perfect,* Samuel decides. He pulls out his flask, ready to anoint Eliab, but God stops him.

"This is not my king," God says. "I am not impressed by what he looks like. It's what is on the inside that counts."

Jesse calls his son Abinadab and introduces him to Samuel. "Not this one," God says. Shimea is next. "Not this one either," God tells

Samuel. All seven of Jesse's sons are introduced to Samuel, and all seven are rejected by God.

Samuel is confused. God told him that one of Jesse's sons was the chosen one. "Um, are these all the sons you have?" Samuel asks Jesse.

"I have one more," Jesse admits. "The youngest is out in the field tending to the sheep."

"Hurry up and call him," Samuel says.

A short time later, a young boy runs through the fields toward the men. He is sweating and breathing hard, but he is still handsome like his brothers. "This is David," Jesse says.

God tells Samuel that David is the one. "God has chosen you to be the next king of Israel," Samuel says to David. Jesse and his other sons stare at David in disbelief. David kneels, and Samuel takes out his flask of oil and pours it on David's head.

Some time later, Jesse gets a message from King Saul. Jesse trembles as he goes to meet the messenger. Has Saul heard that Samuel anointed David as king? Is Saul angry?

"The king asks that you send your youngest son, David, to the palace," the messenger tells Jesse.

"Why?" Jesse asks. His mouth is so dry that he can barely speak. "What do you want with David?"

The LORD doesn't see things the way you see them. People judge by outward appearance, but the LORD looks at the heart.

1 Samuel 16:7

PARK HERE!

READ AND MEMORIZE THIS VERSE.

"King Saul has heard that David is a talented harp player. The king wishes to hear him play."

Jesse lets out a quiet sigh of relief. "I will send David to the king immediately," he promises.

David loves to play the harp and sing. He writes his own songs. Many of them are songs of praise to God.

David takes his harp, goes into the palace, and plays his music for King Saul. The king is often sad and angry, but David's music makes him feel better. Saul loves David's playing so much that he asks Jesse to let David remain in his service.

To learn more about David's anointing, read 1 Samuel 16.

David Faces a Giant Obstacle

David goes back and forth between Saul's palace and his home in Bethlehem. When the king doesn't need him, he helps his father with the sheep. His father needs extra help because David's three oldest brothers are fighting in King Saul's army against the Philistines. One day, Jesse hands David a basket of bread, grain, and cheese. "Take this food to your brothers," he says. David is excited to go. He has never been to a battleground before. When he arrives, he sees King Saul's soldiers standing in battle position on a hill. The Philistine soldiers stand on the opposite hill.

David watches as the ranks of the Philistine army separate. A huge giant, in full armor, walks out from the middle of the Philistine army. He is nine feet tall and carries an enormous sword and spear. The giant laughs at the Israelite army.

"Who will fight me?" the giant hollers. David notices that no one volunteers. Some of the Israelite soldiers even run away in fear. "Come on, send your mightiest warrior! Let's see what the Israelites are made of!" the giant yells again. King Saul's men tremble and glance at each other nervously. "Choose one man to fight me. If he wins, we will be your slaves. But if I win, you will be our slaves!" the giant says.

"Who is this Philistine?" David asks the soldiers standing near him.

"That's Goliath," the soldiers reply. "He's a mighty warrior. He has been taunting us for 40 days. We are all afraid to fight him, because we would surely lose. No one can beat him."

God will help me beat him, David thinks.

King Saul hears that someone is asking about the giant. He sends for David.

"Don't worry about Goliath, Your Majesty," David says. "I will fight him!"

"Don't be silly." Saul shakes his head. "You're only a boy."

"I have fought lions and bears to protect my father's sheep," David says. "God protected me from them, and he'll protect me from Goliath, too!"

Saul finally agrees and offers David his armor to wear. David tries it on, but it is way too big. David can hardly move underneath the heavy armor. "I can't wear this," David tells King Saul. "I have my best weapon right here." He pulls out his slingshot and collects five stones from a nearby stream. The stones feel smooth between his fingers.

David walks toward the giant. Goliath laughs when he sees David coming. "Is this the best you can do, Israel?" he yells. "Am I a dog? Is that why you've sent a boy with a stick after me?"

David stands his ground. "Goliath, you come at me with a sword, spear, and javelin. But I have a much more powerful weapon—God! The Lord will defeat you today."

As Goliath comes to attack, David runs to meet him. He takes a stone from his bag and loads it in his sling, whirling it around and around. The stone flies out of the sling and strikes Goliath right between the eyes. The giant falls facedown on the ground. "Victory!" the Israelites shout. The Philistines can't believe their eyes. A boy has beaten their champion. Terrified, they turn and run. The Israelites chase after them.

To learn more about David and Goliath, read 1 Samuel 17.

"So when does David become king?" Munch asks.

"Not until after Saul dies," Lana says. "Saul gets jealous of all of David's success. For many years, Saul tries to kill David, but David does not fight back. David is a good king, although he also makes a lot of mistakes. But God forgives him. God calls David a man after his own heart."

"A note on the map says that David was the one who made Jerusalem the capital of Israel," Griffin says. "And that's where we're going next."

King David reigns over Israel for a very long time. After he dies, his son Solomon becomes king. Like David, King Solomon is loyal to God. One night, God appears to Solomon in a dream. "Ask me for anything you want, and I will give it to you," God tells Solomon.

"You've blessed me so much already," Solomon answers. "But there IS something I still need—wisdom. Ruling over the people is a hard job. I have to make difficult decisions, and sometimes I don't know the right answers. If I had wisdom, then I would know right from wrong and I could govern your people well."

Jerusalem

God is happy with Solomon's request. "Because

you asked me for wisdom so you can help my people instead of asking for riches or fame or a long life for yourself, I will grant your request," God says. "And I will also give you the things you did not ask for. You will be very wealthy and famous and will have a long life."

One day, Solomon's wisdom is put to the test.

Two women appear before the king, tugging at a baby. "He's my baby!" one woman says.

"No, he's mine!" the other woman says.

"What's going on?" King Solomon interrupts.

"Your Majesty," the first woman says, "this woman and I live in the same house. She stole my baby because her baby died."

"You're lying!" the other woman shrieks. "The baby is mine! SHE stole him from ME!" The women keep arguing, getting louder and louder. They are so busy fighting that they do not even hear the baby's cries.

"Quiet!" King Solomon orders. "Bring me a sword." Someone brings the king a sword, and everyone waits to see what he will do with it. "Let's cut the child in two," King Solomon says. "Each of you can have half. Problem solved." He takes the sword out of its sheath.

"Okay, that sounds fair," one of the women says. "If we can't agree on whose he is, then he won't belong to either of us."

BUILD YOUR FAITH!

Solomon knew that wisdom would help him more than all the treasure in the world. Wisdom is knowing the right thing to do. True wisdom comes from God, and the Bible tells us that he will give it to us when we ask for it (see James 1:5). Is it ever difficult for you to make the right choice? Have you asked God for wisdom?

JERUSALEM

- Jerusalem is the capital of ancient and modern Israel. It became the capital of Israel during the reign of King David.
- Jerusalem was built on a rocky plateau surrounded by hills and valleys. This location protected the city from enemy attacks.
- Solomon built the first Temple in Jerusalem. He used only the finest materials in order to show off the wealth and power of the city. The Temple was destroyed when the Babylonians conquered Judah and rebuilt when the exiles returned to Jerusalem. Years later, King Herod renovated it. It was destroyed a final time by the Romans.
- Houses in Jerusalem were usually made out of mud brick and had a flat roof. Most houses had a small garden and were built near a well.
- Typical food included bread, onions, milk, cheese, legumes, honey, figs, dates, olives, and pomegranates.
- Jerusalem is a holy city in Christianity, Judaism, and Islam.

Fun Fact: In ancient Jerusalem, people ate with their fingers and sat on the floor to dine. Wealthy people sometimes ate on couches. It has been suggested that Jesus and his disciples ate on couches during the Last Supper.

But the child's real mother loves him very much and can't stand to think of him being harmed. "No!" she cries out. "Please don't hurt the baby, Your Majesty! Give her the child, but please don't hurt him!"

"And now the problem really is solved," King Solomon says. "Give the baby to the woman who doesn't want him to be hurt. She is his real mother." The mother holds her baby close and hushes his crying. Everyone in the kingdom is impressed by King Solomon's wisdom.

To learn more about Solomon, read 1 Kings 3.

King of the Mountain

The bus leaves Jerusalem, and Solomon's palace grows smaller and smaller in the distance. Soon, the bus begins to shake as it climbs uphill. "Hold on tight," Griffin says. "This road is bumpy."

"Where are we going?" Munch asks, gripping the seat in front of him.

"To the top of Mount Carmel," Griffin says.

"To see the prophet Elijah," Lana adds, closing the Bible. The kids look out the window as the bus reaches the summit. They see Elijah kneeling in prayer.

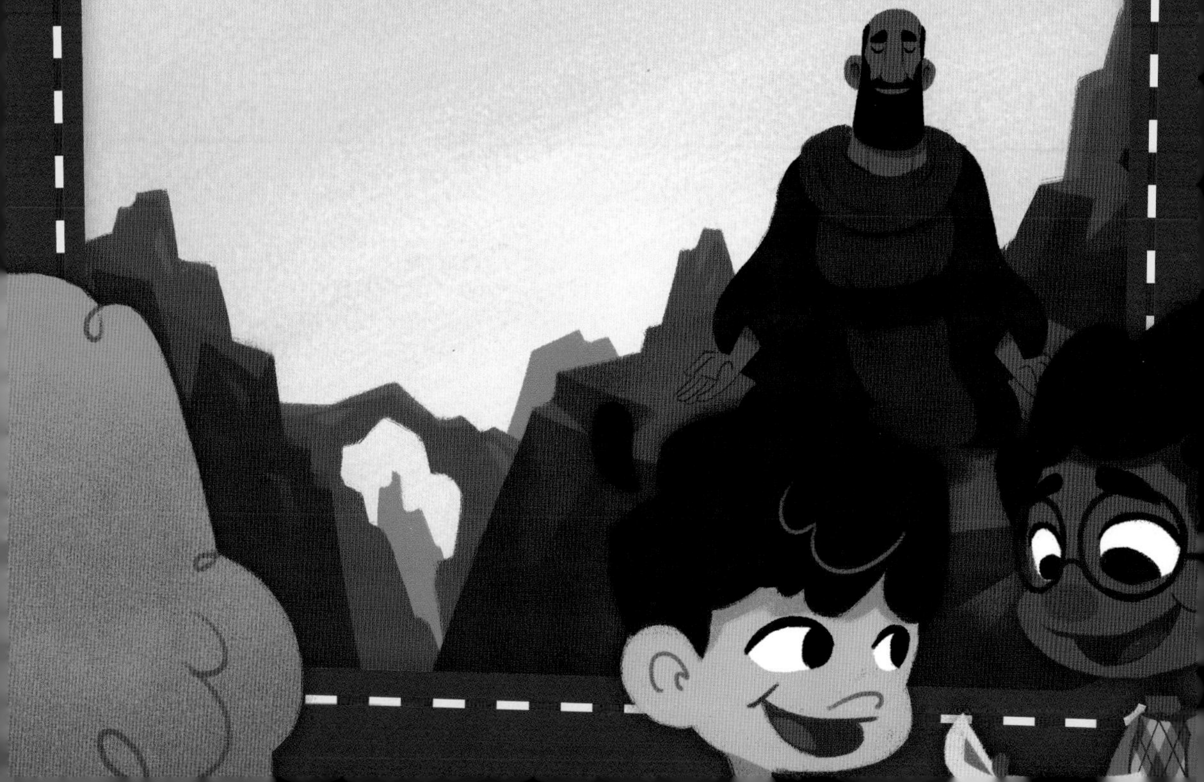

MOUNT CARMEL

- Mount Carmel is a limestone mountain range located in modern-day Palestine, in northern Israel. It extends southeast from the Mediterranean Sea.
- Mount Carmel is a symbol of beauty and fertility.
- It rains a lot on Mount Carmel, making the land fertile. Vegetation grows on the mountainside.

Fun Fact: There are many natural caves on Mount Carmel. Sometimes the prophet Elijah resided in these caves.

Elijah is one of God's prophets. Many years have passed since Solomon was king. The nation has split into two kingdoms, Israel and Judah. Very few of the kings that came after Solomon followed God. King Ahab is one of the worst. He and his wife, Queen Jezebel, worship a fake god named Baal. Jezebel hates the true God so much that she is trying to kill all of his prophets, including Elijah.

Men, women, and children climb Mount Carmel and join Elijah at the summit until all the people of Israel are standing there. Elijah had told King Ahab to call this meeting on top of the mountain.

As the crowd grows, a whisper spreads among them. "Why are we here?" they ask each other.

Elijah finishes his prayer. He stands up and turns toward the people. "How much longer will we debate who the true God is—my Lord or Baal?" Elijah says. "Who's up for a contest?"

There is silence. Then someone shouts out, "What kind of contest?"

"Let's make two sacrifices," Elijah says. "I will bring an offering to the Lord, and Ahab's prophets can bring one to Baal. We will each make an offering of a bull, and then we will pray. The God who answers by setting the altar on fire is the true God."

Everyone agrees, and the contest is on. "We will go first," the prophets of Baal say. They prepare their sacrifice and place it on the altar. Then they begin to cry out to Baal. "O Baal, please send fire!" they pray. But nothing happens. The prophets dance wildly around their altar all morning. But still nothing happens.

THINK ABOUT IT!

Elijah . . . told King Ahab, "As surely as the LORD, the God of Israel, lives—the God I serve—there will be no dew or rain during the next few years until I give the word!"

1 Kings 17:1

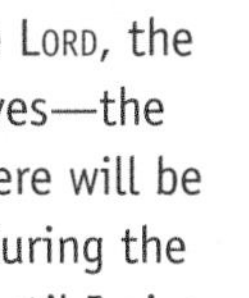

King Ahab and Queen Jezebel worshiped Baal, a false god. Ahab and Jezebel believed that Baal controlled the rain and made the crops grow. The Lord stopped rain from falling on Israel and sent a famine to show them that he was the one in charge of the weather, not Baal. The drought lasted for nearly three years, until God sent rain again.

SLOW!

"You'd better shout louder," Elijah teases. "Maybe Baal is daydreaming, or maybe he's asleep!" Baal's prophets shout louder and even cut themselves with knives and swords to try to get his attention. But nothing happens at all.

"My turn," Elijah says finally. He calls to the people, "Come over here!" All the people watch as Elijah repairs an old altar to the Lord. He digs a big trench around the altar and then puts wood and his sacrifice on top. Then he asks some people to pour water on the sacrifice and the altar until the whole thing is soaked and the trench is full of water. Elijah walks up to the altar and prays, "O Lord, please show all these people that you are really God." Instantly, God's fire falls from heaven and engulfs the altar in flames! The fire burns up the sacrifice, the wood, the stones of the altar, and the dust around the altar. It even dries up all the water in the trench!

All the people on the mountain are astonished. They immediately bow down and worship Elijah's true God.

To learn more about Elijah, read 1 Kings 18.

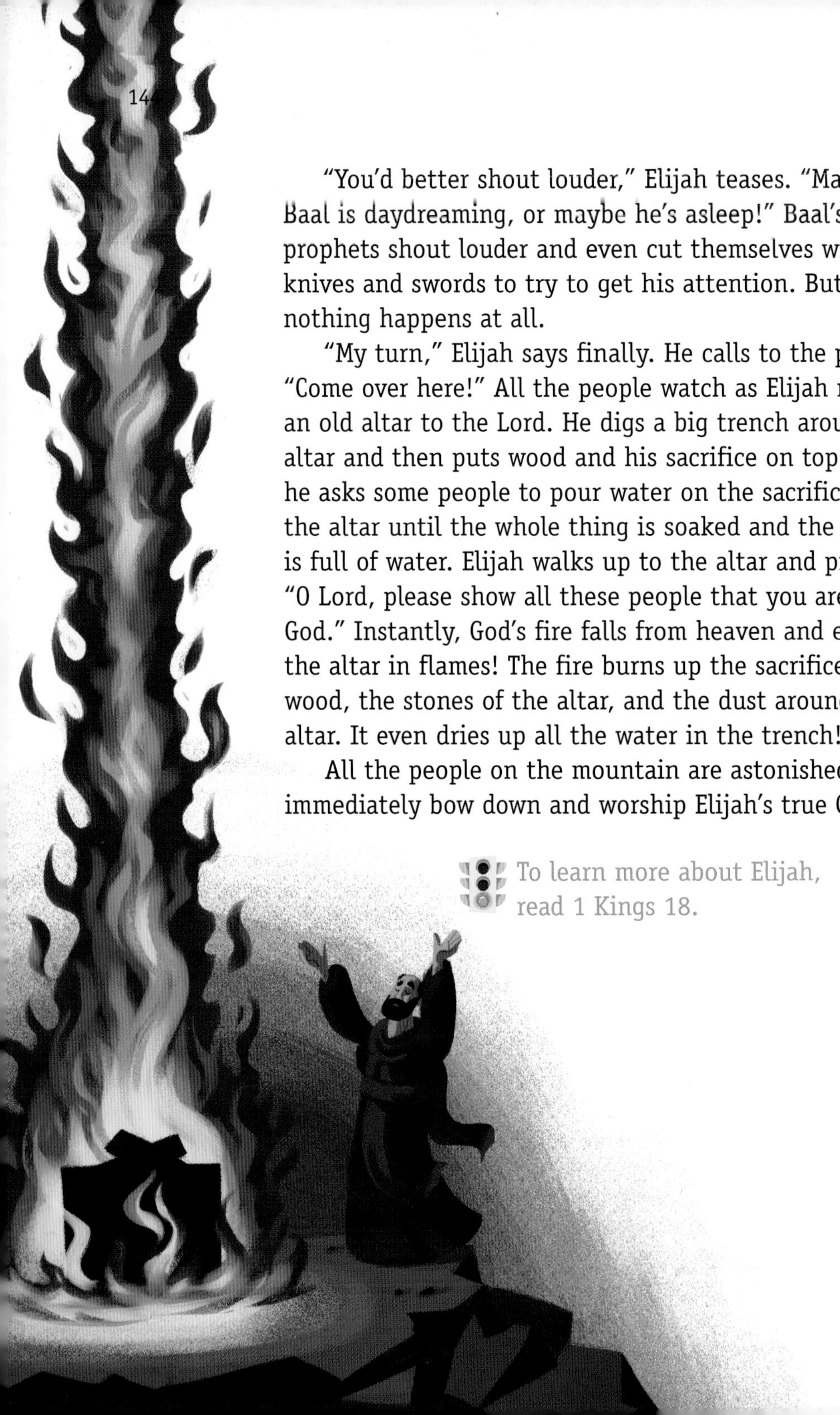

A Whirlwind Trip to Heaven

The bus rattles down the opposite side of Mount Carmel. "Hold on," Griffin says, bracing himself against the seat. When the ride gets a bit smoother, he grabs the map to check out the next stop. "We're headed east," he says, "back to the Jordan River."

A group of 50 men has gathered some distance away from the bank of the Jordan River. Some of them whisper excitedly to each other, while others stand quietly, not taking their eyes off the two men who are coming to the river's edge.

"There's Elijah!" someone says. The words are repeated throughout the group of prophets. "And there's Elisha, his student, with him." The men know that God will take Elijah into heaven today. They are waiting to see how it will happen.

The prophets watch as Elijah and Elisha approach the river. Elijah reaches down and dips his hand in the cool water. Then he does something extraordinary. He removes his cloak and folds it across his arm. He pauses a few seconds and then strikes the water with the cloak. In the exact place where the river was hit, the water parts and a dry path forms. Elijah and Elisha walk across the dry ground to the other side of the river. The prophets watching are amazed.

Elijah and Elisha continue walking for a while. Then Elijah stops and puts his arm around Elisha. "Tell me, before I go to heaven, what can I do for you?" he asks. Elijah knows that Elisha will be a prophet after him and carry on his work. He wants to help him in any way he can.

"Please let me inherit a double share of your spirit," Elisha says. Elisha really wants the Holy Spirit that fills Elijah so that he can do a good job as prophet.

"Well, that's a difficult request," Elijah says. "In order to inherit my spirit, you must see me rise into heaven. If you miss it, you will not get what you asked for."

"I will not leave your side," Elisha says. The men keep walking.

All of a sudden, something catches Elisha's eye.

A chariot of fire shoots out of the sky. It zooms toward the men. The chariot dashes between the two men, separating them. Then, a funnel cloud appears. It whips up dust from the ground, scoops up Elijah, and whisks him up into heaven. Elisha watches the whole thing in awe.

When Elisha finally turns to go, he sees something on the ground. It is Elijah's cloak. Elisha bends over and carefully picks it up.

Elisha folds the cloak over his arm and walks back toward the river. He strikes the water, just as Elijah did. The river parts, and Elisha walks back across the Jordan River toward the group of prophets that are waiting for him. "Here comes Elisha," one of the prophets says. Everyone can see that Elisha is filled with the Holy Spirit.

To learn more about Elijah being taken to heaven, read 2 Kings 2:1-15.

A Sick Visitor

A thick fog rises from the river and blankets the bus in white. "Spinning sprockets!" Munch says. "I can't see a thing." Munch, Lana, and Griffin rub at the windows, but it doesn't help much. They wait for the fog to clear.

"Look! Someone's coming!" Lana says. The children watch as a group of men approach the river. They are dressed in armor, but one man wears armor that is much fancier than the others'.

"That must be the general," Griffin says.

"What's wrong with his skin?" Munch asks.

"Ugh! Look at that muddy water!" the general says in disgust, stopping some distance away from the river. "I'm not bathing in that filth."

"But, General Naaman," a soldier pleads, "Elisha said this was the only cure."

Naaman is the general of the Syrian army, and

he suffers from a terrible skin disease called leprosy. He came all the way to Israel to meet with the prophet Elisha, hoping to be cured.

Naaman has been to Israel before—to raid the land, taking Israelites as captives. One of the prisoners his army took was a young girl. The girl was given to Naaman's wife as a maid. This young girl told Naaman's wife about the great prophet Elisha in the land of Israel. The girl was sure that Elisha would be able to heal Naaman's leprosy.

"I thought that Elisha would heal my leprosy instantly by waving his hand or saying a prayer!" Naaman yells at his officers. They scurry along beside him, trying to keep up with his angry pacing. "But he didn't even come to the door! He sent a servant to tell me to dip myself seven times in this disgusting Jordan River! Doesn't he know who I am?"

The officers look at each other anxiously. "Sir," one pants, "if Elisha had asked you to do something very difficult in order to be healed, wouldn't you have done it? But bathing in this river is an easy thing to do."

"Why not try it?" asks another officer. "You have nothing to lose." Naaman thinks this over.

"Oh, fine!" Naaman says. "Let's just get this over with." He strips off his uniform and jumps into the river. *Splash!* "I hope I don't regret

this!" he yells. Naaman dunks himself in the water seven times, just as Elisha had told him. When he comes out of the water the last time, his skin is completely healed! It is as fresh and smooth as a baby's. The soldiers on the bank stare at him. Their mouths hang open. "What are you gawking at?" Naaman shouts.

"Sir, your skin . . ." a soldier says. Naaman looks down at his arms and legs. The angry expression disappears from his face and is replaced with a huge smile. His eyes fill with tears.

"I'm cured!" Naaman shouts. "My skin is cured!" Naaman's soldiers cheer. "We must go back to Elisha's house," Naaman orders. "He deserves a proper thank you." The entire troop marches back to Elisha's house to thank the prophet. This time, Elisha comes out to see them. "Now I know that the God of Israel is the only true God," Naaman tells Elisha.

To learn more about Elisha and Naaman, read 2 Kings 5.

Voyage to the Belly of a Fish

"Spinning sprockets!" Munch says. "God's power is incredible!"

"If you thought that was cool, wait until you see what God does to Jonah," Lana says. "We're going to Joppa next."

"That's right," Griffin says. "How did you know?"

"Just a hunch," Lana says with a wink. She sets the Bible next to her on the seat.

A little while later, the bus pulls up to a wooden dock. A ship is about to embark. Suddenly, a skinny man with a gray beard runs up the gangplank.

"Hold the boat!" the man yells. The sailors wait impatiently for him to get on. The man jumps onto the deck and bends over, hands on his knees. "You're going to Tarshish, right?" he pants.

"That's right," a sailor says. "It's going to be a long journey."

"Perfect," the man says. "I need to get far away from here." The man's name is Jonah, and he is running away from God.

God wants Jonah to travel to Nineveh, the capital of the Assyrian Empire.

Nineveh

Tarshish

God wants Jonah to tell the Assyrians that if they don't stop doing evil things, God will destroy their city. But Jonah doesn't want to go to Nineveh. Jonah plans to sail in the opposite direction, and FAST!

God doesn't let Jonah get away with disobeying him. He sends a powerful wind to blow over the sea, whipping up a terrifying storm.

The sky turns black. Wave after wave crashes against the boat, splashing water onto the deck. The sailors are terrified. "We're going to sink!" a sailor shouts. "The waves are too large!" Jonah holds on tightly to a cargo net so he won't be swept into the sea. He knows the storm is his fault. *Maybe I should have listened to God,* he thinks.

As the boat rocks from side to side, the sailors hold on to any object they can find. "What is causing this horrible storm?" they ask.

Jonah can't keep quiet anymore. "I am the cause of the storm," he tells the sailors. "I serve the one true God. He made this ocean, and I have disobeyed him. Throw me overboard, and then my God will calm the sea."

The sailors glance at each other anxiously. They don't want to throw someone overboard. So they do their best to row to land, but the sea is too wild. "We have to do something," one sailor shouts, "or else this boat will soon be at the bottom of the ocean!"

"We have no choice," another sailor says. "Let's do what that man, Jonah, said. Throw him overboard." The men say a prayer for forgiveness, and then they toss Jonah high into the air. He splashes into the deep, dark water. It's freezing—so cold that Jonah can hardly swim. *I'm going to drown,* Jonah thinks. *This is the end.*

JOPPA

- Joppa was an ancient seaport along the Mediterranean Sea. Today, it is called Jaffa.
- Joppa was a prominent seaport for ancient Jerusalem, as it was located approximately 40 miles away.
- When Solomon built his Temple, he brought the wood cut in Lebanon through the port of Joppa.

Fun Fact: It is believed that Joppa may have been founded by Japheth, the son of Noah.

NINEVEH

- Nineveh was a city located near the Tigris River on a fertile plain. It was the capital of the Assyrian Empire.
- The city had parks, a library, large buildings, and gardens. It also had a huge defensive wall built around it. Nineveh was destroyed in 612 BC by the Babylonians.
- The Assyrians are credited with many inventions, including paved roads, libraries, and plumbing.

Fun Fact: The Bible says that it took three days to see the whole city of Nineveh and that more than 120,000 people lived there.

Just then, a huge fish swims up, opens its mouth, and swallows Jonah whole! "Whoooaaaa!" Jonah cries as he slides down the fish's throat. He comes to a stop inside the fish's belly. It's dark and wet and smells horrible. Bones from the fish's meals poke Jonah every time he moves.

Jonah is in the belly of the fish for three days and three nights. He has a lot of time to think and pray. *What's going to happen to me?* he wonders. *Will I ever get out of here?*

Jonah soon discovers that God still has a plan for him. There is a gurgling sound, and suddenly Jonah shoots out of the fish's mouth. He flies through the air and lands on dry ground with a giant *thud*! "Go to Nineveh, and give them the message I have given you," God orders Jonah again.

This time I'm going to obey God! Jonah thinks. He travels to Nineveh and delivers God's message. The people listen to Jonah and stop doing evil. So God does not destroy the city.

To learn more about Jonah, read the book of Jonah.

Follow the Little Leader

"Wow! What a trip for Jonah," Lana says. "From Joppa toward Tarshish, to the bottom of the sea, and finally to Nineveh!"

"He sure did cover a lot of the map!" Munch jokes.

"But not as much as we're covering!" Griffin says. "We're headed back to Jerusalem again."

The sounds of trumpets and cheering fill the street. It's a day of celebration. A new king is going to be crowned! Crowds of people watch excitedly as a golden crown is brought out and placed on the head of an eight-year-old boy. The boy king, Josiah, waves to the people of Judah. Josiah wants to be a good king who pleases God. His father, King Amon, and grandfather King Manasseh were evil rulers who hurt the people and worshiped fake gods. Josiah has a lot of work to do to get the kingdom of Judah back on track.

Josiah studies hard to learn

how to be a good king. He listens to wise advisers. He reads about King David and tries to follow his example. Most of all, he prays that God would help him lead his people and do what is right.

"It's time to get rid of all these fake gods," Josiah tells the people years later. He gathers some of his soldiers, and they hit the streets of Judah. They destroy all the statues and altars that were built to honor false gods. All carved idols are collected and smashed into bits. "From now on, my people will worship the true God!" Josiah exclaims.

Josiah is also upset about the state of the Lord's Temple, which Solomon had built many years before. No one has been taking care of it for a long time, and it is in bad shape. It looks old, broken down, and dirty. "Let's fix the Temple for our God!" Josiah says. He collects money for the project and gives it to Hilkiah, the high priest. "Use this money to pay workers to rebuild the Temple," Josiah instructs. Hilkiah uses the money honestly, hiring carpenters and builders. While the Temple is being fixed, Hilkiah makes a discovery—a dusty old scroll lying under some rubble.

When he opens the scroll, Hilkiah can hardly believe his eyes. "It's the Book of the Law!" he exclaims. "I'm holding God's words!" Hilkiah rushes to bring the scroll to the king's palace.

King Josiah orders his secretary to read him the scroll. When he hears what is written in it, Josiah rips his clothing to show deep sadness. "Oh, how we have dishonored God!" Josiah cries. "We have disobeyed the laws that he gave us."

King Josiah doesn't waste any time. He calls for all the people in his kingdom to come to a meeting.

"Everyone come to the Temple," he says. "I want to read you God's laws." Josiah holds the scroll high above his head. "These words were given to Moses by God." Josiah reads the entire Book of the Law to the people. It is the first time many of them have ever heard God's words. Then Josiah makes a promise to the Lord. "I promise to obey the Lord by keeping all his commands, laws, and decrees with all my heart and soul," he says. All the people make the same promise.

To learn more about Josiah, read 2 Kings 22–23.

Four Friends Far from Home

The bus leaves Jerusalem and drives toward Babylon. It enters the busy city and stops in front of a splendid palace. The children watch as a line of young men walk through the front doors. They are all handsome and wear fine clothes. Four of them stand close together. They put their heads together and talk softly. "I bet that's Daniel and his friends," Lana whispers.

"Daniel!" one of the young men, Mishael, whispers to his friend. "We can't eat this food!"

"This table is full of things God has told us not to eat," their friend Azariah agrees. "And the rest of it was probably offered to idols."

"But what can we do?" Hananiah, the fourth young man, asks. "King Nebuchadnezzar wants us to be like the Babylonians now."

Nebuchadnezzar, the king of Babylon, has conquered the four friends' homeland of Judah. He has brought back some of the young men from Judah's wealthiest families to train them to serve in his court. He wants the young men to do everything the way the Babylonians do. He has even given them Babylonian names—he changed Daniel's name to Belteshazzar; and Hananiah, Mishael, and Azariah are now to be called Shadrach, Meshach, and Abednego.

Daniel looks at the king's food, then looks back at his friends. He stands up straight and lifts his head high. "God is still God here in Babylon," he says. "We must follow his rules no matter where we are."

Hananiah, Mishael, and Azariah nod. They stand up straight and tall.

"There's Ashpenaz, the king's chief officer," Daniel says. "Let's talk to him about the food."

Ashpenaz likes Daniel and his friends, but his face turns pale when he hears their request. "You have to eat this food!" Ashpenaz exclaims. "It's from the king's own table—the best our land has to offer! If you don't eat the food, you will get skinny and weak. Then I will get in big trouble with the king!"

"Maybe we could do a little test," Daniel suggests. "Feed my friends and me vegetables and water for 10 days, and compare us to the other young men. Then you can make a decision based on what you see."

Ashpenaz agrees. For 10 days, he secretly gives Daniel, Hananiah, Mishael, and Azariah only vegetables and water. At the end of the 10 days, Ashpenaz is amazed. Daniel and his friends look healthier and stronger

than all of the other young men. "How can this be?" he asks Daniel. "From now on, you may have any food you ask for!"

After the young men have finished their training, Ashpenaz brings them all to King Nebuchadnezzar. The king speaks to all of them to see how well they have learned their lessons. "Belteshazzar, Shadrach, Meshach, and Abednego are the smartest and wisest young men in this whole group!" King Nebuchadnezzar says to Ashpenaz. "I will give them important jobs in my court."

Some time later, King Nebuchadnezzar builds a huge statue out of gold and sets it up in a large field. "Everyone must worship this new god!" he proclaims. "When you hear the sound of music, bow down to the statue. If you don't, you will be thrown into a fiery furnace."

Hananiah, Mishael, and Azariah are standing together in the field. They turn and look at each other. "There is only one God," Azariah says.

Mishael nods. "We will not worship a false god, even if it means we have to die," he says. Hananiah puts his hands on his friends' shoulders.

BUILD YOUR FAITH!

Daniel, Hananiah, Mishael, and Azariah stood up for what they knew was right, even though it would have been much easier to go along with what everyone else was doing. Have you ever been in a situation where the people you were with were all doing something you knew was wrong? What did you do? Pray that the next time you are in a situation like that, God will give you the same courage that he gave to Daniel and his friends.

When the music plays, everyone bows and worships the king's gold statue. But Hananiah, Mishael, and Azariah stand tall.

Soon the three friends are caught and brought before the king. Nebuchadnezzar's face is red with anger. "Shadrach, Meshach, and Abednego!" he shouts. "What is this I hear about you refusing to worship my statue?"

"There is only one God, Your Majesty," the three friends say. "And he is powerful enough to save us from your punishment. But even if he doesn't, we will never worship that statue."

King Nebuchadnezzar's face turns from red to purple. "Make the furnace seven times hotter than usual," he roars. "Throw them into the fire!"

The king's soldiers tie up the three friends and throw them into the furnace. The fire is so hot that it kills the soldiers when they get close! Hananiah, Mishael, and Azariah fall into the blazing flames.

King Nebuchadnezzar watches his punishment

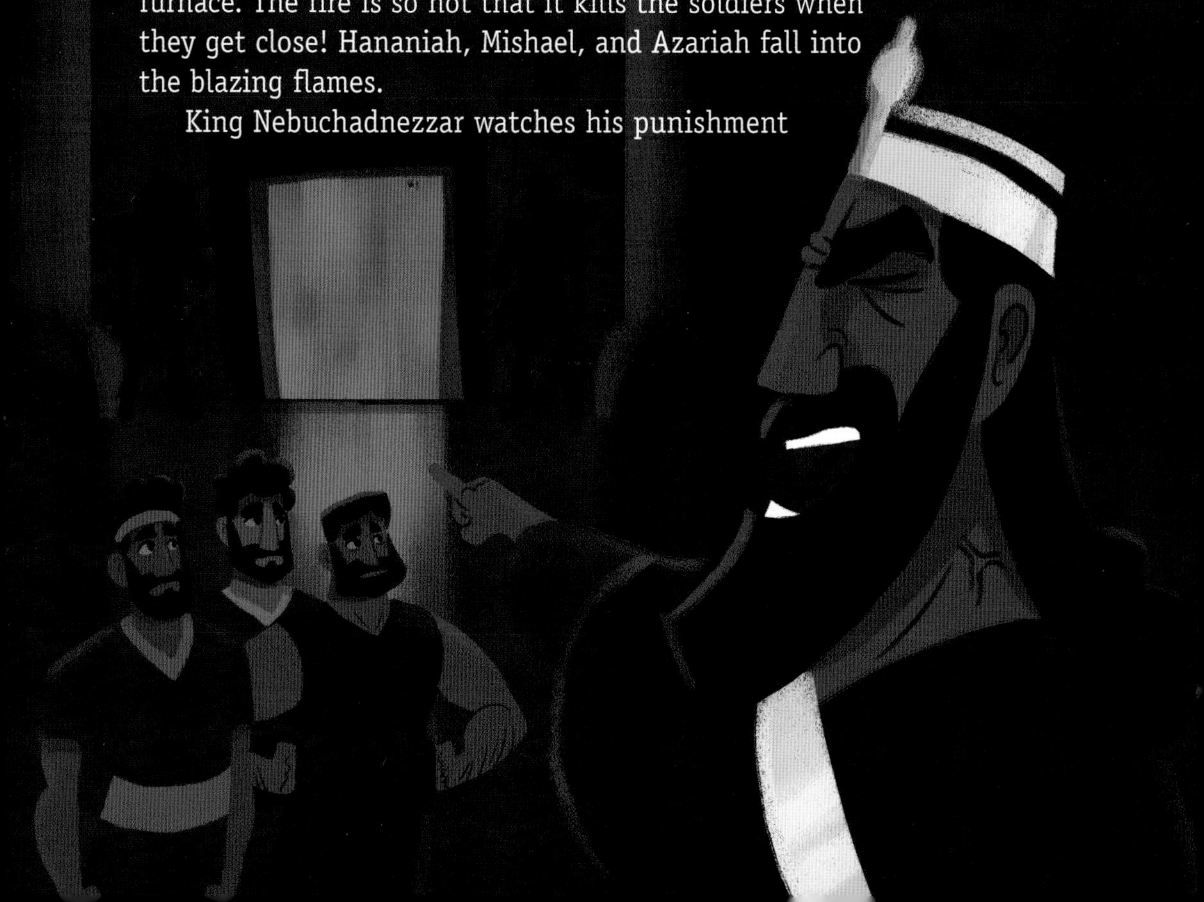

being carried out. But suddenly he cries out and leaps to his feet. "Wait a minute!" he yells to his advisers. "Didn't we throw three men into the furnace?"

"Yes, Your Majesty," the advisers reply.

"Then why are there FOUR men walking around in there? They aren't tied up. They aren't burning. They're just walking around! And one of them looks like a god!"

Nebuchadnezzar creeps as close as he can to the furnace. "Shadrach, Meshach, and Abednego," he yells. "Come out!"

The three friends walk out of the furnace. They have not been harmed at all by the flames. They don't even smell like smoke.

"Praise the God of Shadrach, Meshach, and Abednego!" the king exclaims. "No other god is like him."

To learn more about Daniel and his three friends, read Daniel 1–3.

An Overnight Stop in a Den of Lions

Daniel kneels on the floor of his upstairs room. His gray head is bowed, and his wrinkled hands are gently folded in prayer. He enjoys the breeze from the open window as a gust of wind dances past his cheek and snuffs out his candle.

"Thank you, God, for another day of life," Daniel prays. "Thank you for watching over me and allowing me to serve you even in Babylon."

Daniel has served several kings of Babylon. King Nebuchadnezzar has been dead for years, and Daniel is now an important adviser to King Darius. Daniel helps the king and is the boss of all the king's other advisers and officers. He is very good at his job. But the other advisers are terribly jealous of Daniel. For a long time, they have been looking for a way to get him in trouble. "Daniel is too good," they said. "We will have to find a way to use his faith in God against him." So today, they went to King Darius and tricked him into signing a new law. It says that for 30 days, no one is allowed to pray to anyone other than the king. If they do, they will be thrown into a den filled with hungry lions.

When Daniel hears about the new law, he sighs. But then he goes home and goes upstairs to his room, just like always. "I pray to God three times a day, every day," Daniel says to himself. "And I will continue to do what is right." Then he kneels down like he's always done.

As Daniel finishes his prayer, there is a knock at his door. "Lord, please give me courage," Daniel says. Then he goes downstairs to answer the door.

The advisers who tricked the king barge into Daniel's home. "There he is!" one of them shouts. "We saw you through your window. You were praying to God, breaking the law of King Darius."

The advisers drag Daniel to the king's palace. "Your Majesty, we found your favorite helper, Daniel, breaking your law today," they sneer. "He was praying to God!"

King Darius is horrified and angry when he realizes how he has been tricked. He likes Daniel and relies on his advice. He doesn't want to lose his best helper. The king spends the rest of the day trying to figure out a way to save Daniel. In the evening, the king's advisers come to pester him. "Your Majesty, you signed the law yourself," the advisers remind the king. "There is no way it can be changed." The men smile at each other, and the king sighs.

"I have no choice," he says sadly. "Arrest

THINK ABOUT IT!

Darius the Mede took over the kingdom at the age of sixty-two.

Daniel 5:31

Daniel served as an adviser to several Babylonian kings. Then the Persian Empire conquered Babylon, and Daniel became an adviser to the Persian king Darius. Some believe that "Darius the Mede" was another name for Cyrus, the Persian ruler who conquered Babylon and eventually allowed the Israelite exiles to return to their homeland.

Daniel and throw him into the lions' den." King Darius can barely watch the arrest. "May your God, whom you serve so faithfully, rescue you," he says to Daniel. He closes his eyes as Daniel is tossed to the lions and the den is sealed shut with a heavy rock. Then the king races back to his palace. He locks himself inside and weeps for Daniel. He doesn't eat or see any visitors all evening.

When the first ray of morning light hits his window, the king jumps out of bed. He dashes to the lions' den. Wringing his hands, he calls out, "Daniel, did your God rescue you?" The king holds his breath, listening.

"Long live the king!" Daniel answers. "God sent an angel to shut the lions' mouths so they would not hurt me."

King Darius almost collapses from relief and joy. "Get Daniel out at once!" he orders. Daniel is lifted out of the den. The king looks Daniel over from head to toe. There is not a scratch on him.

To learn more about Daniel in the lions' den, read Daniel 6.

O Lord, you are a great and awesome God! You always fulfill your covenant and keep your promises of unfailing love to those who love you and obey your commands.

Daniel 9:4

PARK HERE!

READ AND MEMORIZE THIS VERSE.

A Very Long Walk for a Queen

Lana, Griffin, and Munch stare out the window at Daniel with their mouths hanging open. "Spinning sprockets!" Munch whispers. The bus starts up, and they sit back in their seats. No one says a word for a long time.

When the bus passes a sign that reads Persia, Griffin speaks up. "I think we've arrived at our next stop," he says. "Welcome to Persia."

A beautiful girl looks out the window of her palace. She is dressed in clothes made of the finest fabrics and wears expensive gold jewelry. Touching the crown that sits on her head, she says, "I still can't believe King Xerxes chose me, a Jewish girl, to be the queen of Persia. What will cousin Mordecai say?"

When King Xerxes sent his old queen away, he brought all the pretty young girls of his kingdom, including Esther, to live at the palace. Each day, the girls were given beauty treatments and new dresses. Every girl tried to impress

Xerxes, hoping to become the new queen. The king chose Esther to be his new bride.

Esther is glad that her cousin Mordecai works in the palace and can come to visit her every now and then. Mordecai is like a father to Esther. When her parents died, he adopted her and raised her as his own daughter. Mordecai hears many interesting things in his job as a palace official. Once he even hears that someone is planning to kill the king! Mordecai tells Esther about the plot, and she warns the king, saving his life.

One day Mordecai brings Esther some very bad news. "Haman, the king's most powerful official, hates our people, the Jews. He is coming up with a plan to kill us all."

"Oh, no!" Esther gasps. "What should we do?"

"You are the only one who can save us," Mordecai tells her. "You must go and ask the king to help the Jewish people."

PERSIA

- Persia was an Asian empire that extended from India to Ethiopia. It is located in modern-day Iran.
- The Persians conquered the Babylonian Empire in 539 BC, nearly 50 years before Esther was born.
- Persians ate apricots, lemons, limes, eggplant, yogurt, rice, meat, pomegranates, nuts, and other fruits and vegetables. They lived in mud brick houses that often had a pond or fountain nearby.
- King Xerxes's palace was located in Susa, the capital of Persia.

Fun Fact: The Persian Empire was built and expanded by Cyrus the Great in the sixth century BC.

Esther is very quiet. "If I go to the king without being invited, he might punish me, even kill me."

"You must be brave, Esther," Mordecai says. "You became queen for this very reason."

Esther lifts her chin and straightens her shoulders. "Gather our people together," she tells Mordecai. "Pray for me for three days. After that, I will go see the king, even though it is against the law. If I must die, I must die."

Three days later, Esther puts on her most beautiful clothes and her royal crown. She walks through the palace to the king's inner court, trying not to think about what might happen. "One foot in front of the other. One step at a time," she whispers to herself.

Finally she reaches the king's court. Esther takes a deep breath and enters the room. The king is sitting on his throne, facing the entrance. Esther sees the king notice her, and she holds her breath, waiting to see what he will do.

BUILD YOUR FAITH!

Esther was very afraid to go see the king without being invited—and with good reason! She knew that she might be killed if she went. But she decided to go anyway, because she knew it was right to stand up for others being persecuted. Sometimes standing up for someone being bullied or picked on can be a scary thing. You might even be afraid the bully will start picking on you. Ask God for the courage to do the right thing, and stand up for others when they need help.

The king smiles. "Welcome, Queen Esther!" he says. "Come here, my love." He holds out his gold scepter to Esther, signaling that she is allowed to come close to him. Esther walks over to the king and touches the end of the scepter, letting out a huge sigh of relief.

"What do you need, my queen?" the king asks. "I will give you anything you ask for."

Esther has a plan. She invites the king and Haman to a private party with her. They gladly accept her invitation. Esther serves rich food and drinks, and everyone has a wonderful time.

"This was an excellent party, Esther," the king says, rubbing his stomach. "But what did you really want to talk to me about?"

Esther smiles at the king. "Please, Your Majesty, would you and

Haman come to another party tomorrow? Then I will tell you what I need."

The king agrees. Haman is puffed up with pride. He can't believe that the queen has invited him to not one but two parties with just her and the king! He goes home and brags about it to all his friends and relatives. "And soon I will get rid of all those disgusting Jews, too!" he says.

At the second banquet, Esther explains the situation to the king. "I would not have bothered you if this weren't a matter of life and death, Your Majesty," she says. "But my people are in very serious danger. There is someone who wants to kill me and all of my people."

This makes the king furious. "Who would dare to threaten my queen?" he roars.

Esther points at Haman. "He would!" she says.

The king is so angry that he can't even speak. He storms out into the garden.

Haman knows that he is doomed. He falls at Esther's feet, begging for his life. "I didn't know you were Jewish!" he sobs. Just then the king comes back inside and sees Haman hanging on to the queen.

"You have the nerve to attack the queen right here in the palace?" he yells. "Guards, take him away!"

The king punishes Haman and makes Mordecai his chief official instead. Esther's courage has saved her people.

To learn more about Esther, read the book of Esther.

The Journey Back to Jerusalem

The bus makes a U-turn and drives toward Jerusalem. A few miles away from the city, the bus joins a huge crowd heading in the same direction. Thousands of men, women, and children walk through what used to be the city gates. They look exhausted and are carrying all of their belongings.

"Look at all of these people!" Munch says.

"What do you think they're doing?" Griffin asks.

"I'm not sure," Lana replies. She pulls out the Bible and flips through the pages. "I think these people have come from Babylon," Lana says. "When King Cyrus of Persia captured Babylon, he told all of the captives being held there that they could return to their homeland and rebuild the Temple."

The kids look around as the bus enters Jerusalem. "This city needs a little work," Munch observes. "Hey, who is that man with the giant scroll?"

"I bet that's Ezra," Lana says.

Jerusalem

The man *is* Ezra. As a priest and scribe, he has spent most of his life writing down and studying the Word of God. Ezra was a captive in Babylon, where he was an official of the king. Now he has come with several thousand other Israelites to Jerusalem to help rebuild the city. When Ezra arrives in Jerusalem, he is not happy with what he finds. He notices that many of the people in Jerusalem are disobeying God. Some families still worship false gods. Other families are doing business on the Sabbath, the day of rest. "No one is following God's laws," Ezra says to himself.

Ezra also checks out the progress the Israelites have made on rebuilding Jerusalem. "Well, at least the Temple construction project is finished," Ezra says. "That's a start. And it's a good thing Nehemiah has come to work on the wall." Ezra's friend Nehemiah was also a captive in Babylon. He served as a cupbearer to King Artaxerxes. One day, when Nehemiah was bringing the king his drink, the king asked

him why he looked so sad. "I am sad because Jerusalem, my home, has been destroyed," Nehemiah told the king. "The city gates have been burned down, and the wall around Jerusalem is no longer standing. My people, the Israelites, cannot even defend their city." Without a city wall, the Israelites were unable to protect themselves from robbers and bandits. The Israelites' enemies wouldn't stop attacking Jerusalem, and there was no way to keep them out.

The king gave Nehemiah permission to leave his royal service. "Go to Jerusalem and rebuild your city," the king ordered. "I will send my army to protect you, and I will pay for the repairs out of the royal treasury."

Nehemiah and his men work hard on building the wall. Their job has been made even harder by enemies who want to stop the Israelites from rebuilding Jerusalem. Nehemiah and his builders have had to rebuild the wall and protect it at the same time.

Ezra and Nehemiah have come to Jerusalem with the same goal.

They both want to see good times come to Jerusalem again. Ezra picks up a large scroll, the Book of the Law, and heads toward the city square. He knows he has an important job to do. He must lead the Israelites back to God. He will teach them to live in a way that pleases the Lord.

All the people of Israel gather in the city square. Ezra stands high above them on a wooden platform and unrolls his giant scroll. The crowd listens silently while Ezra begins to read from the Book of the Law. He reads and reads for hours. The people begin to weep, sad to learn that they have been making poor choices. They want to start obeying God.

When Ezra and Nehemiah hear the sounds of sniffling and crying, they say, "Don't cry or be sad! This is a holy day. We should celebrate." So Ezra takes a break from reading, and all the people celebrate with food, sweet drinks, and dancing.

The next morning, Ezra resumes reading the Book of the Law. He reads the scroll to the people for days, until they have heard every last word of God's law. Then all the people confess their sins. They apologize for everything they have done wrong and promise to start obeying God again. It is a new beginning for Israel.

To learn more about Ezra, Nehemiah, and the return to Israel, read the books of Ezra and Nehemiah.

Gabriel Makes a Special Trip

The wind blows fast and hard. A whirlwind forms and swallows up the bus in a thick cloud of dust. "I can't see a thing," Lana says, frantically wiping at the window.

"Me either," Munch agrees. The bus shakes and jolts with each gust of wind. Then suddenly everything is still. Lana, Griffin, and Munch sit in the deep, quiet darkness. "What's happening?" Munch whispers.

"Don't worry," Griffin says. "I think this is how the bus travels in time."

"We're time traveling again?" Munch asks.

"Well, we just saw a lot of the stories in the Old Testament," Griffin explains. "My guess is that now we are going to see what happens in the New Testament."

"I bet you're right!" Lana says. She watches out the window as the Temple comes into view. It is much larger than before. "We're still in Jerusalem," she says as a man walks across the Temple courtyard.

Zechariah the priest approaches the Holy Place in the Temple. Today, he has been chosen out of many priests to burn incense on the altar in the Holy Place. It is a very important job, and this will probably be the only time in his whole life that Zechariah gets to do it. He doesn't say a word as he carefully prepares the incense and places it on the altar. Soon the smell of perfumed smoke fills the air.

THINK ABOUT IT!

The angel said, "I am Gabriel! I stand in the very presence of God. It was he who sent me to bring you this good news!"
Luke 1:19

Gabriel is one of God's special angels, and one of two angels who are named in the Bible (the other is Michael; see Daniel 10:13). Gabriel delivers important messages for God and appears in the Bible at least three times. He explains a vision to Daniel (see Daniel 9:20-27), tells Zechariah that Elizabeth will have a son, and also brings a young woman named Mary some news about a very special baby.

Suddenly, an angel appears, standing next to the altar! Zechariah gasps and hides his eyes. "Don't be afraid, Zechariah," the angel says. "I have good news." Zechariah looks up at the angel. "Your wife, Elizabeth, is going to have a son," the angel continues. "You will name him John. He will be filled with God's Holy Spirit even before he is born, and he will tell others about the coming of God's Son."

Zechariah can't believe his ears. He and Elizabeth have wished for a child for many years, but they have never been able to have a baby. And now they are very old. "How can I be sure that this will really happen?" he asks.

The angel frowns. "I am Gabriel!" he tells Zechariah. "I stand before God, and he sent me to bring you this wonderful news! But because you didn't believe me, you will not be able to say another word until your baby is born."

Zechariah opens his mouth to answer, but there is no sound. He can't talk! When he leaves the Holy Place, the people outside are anxious. They wonder why Zechariah has taken so long to come out. Zechariah can't say a word to them, but he tries to talk to them with sign language. "Zechariah must have seen something amazing in there!" the people say.

After Zechariah finishes his work in the Temple, he goes home. He tries to think of how to explain to Elizabeth what Gabriel said. When Elizabeth finally understands what Zechariah is trying to tell her, she is so happy that she dances all around the room. "We are finally going to have a baby!" she cries, hugging Zechariah until he thinks he might pop. "It's a miracle!"

Soon, Elizabeth becomes pregnant. "God is so kind," she says. "He has taken away my shame of having no children."

To learn more about Zechariah and Elizabeth, read Luke 1:5-25.

"Wow," Lana whispers.

"Yeah, no kidding. Can you imagine not being able to talk for nine whole months?" Munch asks.

"I meant God giving Zechariah and Elizabeth a baby!" Lana says, giggling. Munch and Griffin join in the laughter as the bus leaves Jerusalem and heads north toward a small town called Nazareth.

A young girl named Mary whistles cheerfully as she goes about her daily chores. She is daydreaming about her fiancé, a strong, young carpenter named Joseph. Soon, they will be married. Mary can hardly wait.

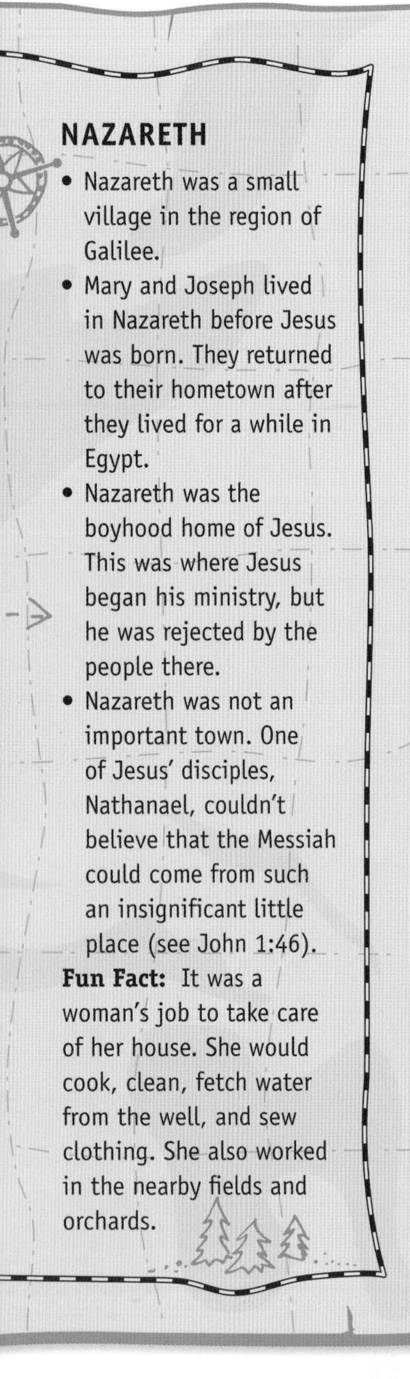

NAZARETH

- Nazareth was a small village in the region of Galilee.
- Mary and Joseph lived in Nazareth before Jesus was born. They returned to their hometown after they lived for a while in Egypt.
- Nazareth was the boyhood home of Jesus. This was where Jesus began his ministry, but he was rejected by the people there.
- Nazareth was not an important town. One of Jesus' disciples, Nathanael, couldn't believe that the Messiah could come from such an insignificant little place (see John 1:46).

Fun Fact: It was a woman's job to take care of her house. She would cook, clean, fetch water from the well, and sew clothing. She also worked in the nearby fields and orchards.

Out of nowhere, an angel appears right in front of Mary! She stumbles backward, nearly falling over a basket. "Hello there, favored woman!" the angel Gabriel says. "The Lord is with you!"

Mary is afraid and confused. "Who are you, and what do you want?" she asks.

"Don't be afraid, Mary," Gabriel says. "God is very happy with you. You are going to be the mother of a very special baby. His name will be Jesus, and he will be King forever."

"I don't understand," Mary says. "How will this be possible?"

"Your child will be the Son of God. The Holy

Spirit will make it possible for you to have a baby," the angel says. "Nothing is impossible with God."

Mary touches her stomach. *Could this really be true?* she wonders. Finally, she speaks. "I am the Lord's servant," Mary says. "I will do whatever God asks."

Gabriel smiles and disappears.

When Joseph hears that Mary is going to have a baby, he feels like his heart will break. He knows that he is not the baby's father. *Mary must have broken her promise to me and fallen in love with another man,* he thinks. *We can't get married now.*

Joseph could break his engagement to Mary in public so that everyone will know that she has done something wrong. But he is a good and kind man, and he doesn't want to embarrass her. "Tomorrow I will go break the engagement privately," he says to himself.

Joseph goes to sleep for the night with tears in his eyes. An angel appears to him in a dream. "Joseph, don't worry about taking Mary as your wife," the angel says. "She has not broken her promise to you. The Holy Spirit has made it possible for her to have this baby.

"Don't be afraid, Mary," the angel told her, "for you have found favor with God! You will conceive and give birth to a son, and you will name him Jesus. He will be very great and will be called the Son of the Most High."

Luke 1:30-32

You must name the baby Jesus, and he will save his people from their sins."

When Joseph wakes up, he runs as fast as he can to Mary's house. He takes her hands in his. "I know that your baby is the Son of God," he says. "I will take care of him and of you."

To learn more about Gabriel's announcements to Mary and Joseph, read Luke 1:26-38 and Matthew 1:18-25.

The One Who Will Prepare the Way

"God gave both Mary and Joseph a lot of faith," Griffin says.

"He sure did," Lana agrees.

The engine chugs and splutters as the bus travels uphill. "We must be following Mary on her trip to visit Elizabeth," Lana says. "Look! There she is!" Lana waves at Mary as the bus passes a group of travelers.

Griffin looks at the map. "We're back in Judea, where Jerusalem is located," he says. "Zechariah and Elizabeth live in a town in the hill country."

Knock! Knock! Mary taps at the door of Elizabeth's home. Elizabeth rushes to see who has come to visit. "Cousin Mary!" she exclaims. "Please come in!" The two women hug.

"It's wonderful to see you, Elizabeth!" Mary says. At the sound of Mary's voice, something amazing

JUDEA

- Judea was a region in the southern part of Israel. Jerusalem is located in Judea.
- Judea is named after Judah, one of Jacob's 12 sons.
- The land in Judea is made up of mountains and deserts. It is barren of vegetation.
- Summers are hot and dry in Judea. Winters are cold and wet.
- Farming was very difficult in Judea because the soil is rocky.
- People in Judea ate lentils, figs, olives, grapes, barley, and wheat. Most lived in houses made of mud brick, though some people had houses made of limestone.
- The Judean wilderness was a place someone went to in order to hide or to be alone.

Fun Fact: The Judean wilderness today looks like what it did in ancient times.

happens. The baby inside Elizabeth leaps for joy, and Elizabeth is filled with God's Holy Spirit.

"God has given you a wonderful gift," Elizabeth tells Mary, putting her hand gently on Mary's belly. "Your child is very special."

Mary smiles. Joy bubbles up inside her until she can't keep it in any longer. She opens her mouth and begins to sing, right there in Elizabeth's doorway. "Oh, how my soul praises the Lord," she sings. "How my spirit rejoices in God my Savior!"

Mary stays with Elizabeth for about three months. They feel very close to each other, since they have both been given miraculous

babies to bring into the world. The two women talk for hours about being pregnant and the plans they have for their children.

Soon the time comes for Elizabeth to give birth to her son. When the baby is a week old, Elizabeth and Zechariah's friends and relatives gather in their home to meet him and hear what his name will be.

"What a beautiful boy!" a woman exclaims.

"God is so good," another woman says, gently touching the baby's head.

"You should name him after his father, Zechariah," a man says. "Every father is proud to have his son named after him."

"No, we are going to name the baby John," Elizabeth says.

"John!" a woman blurts out. "What kind of name is that? Nobody in your family has that name."

"Let's ask his father what he wants to name the baby," someone says.

"Yes!" says another voice. "Zechariah, what do you want your son's name to be?"

Zechariah smiles. Since he is still unable to speak, he reaches for his writing tablet and spells the name he has chosen for his new son. Friends and family crane their necks to see what he is writing.

"Well, let's see it!" somebody shouts.

Zechariah turns the tablet around. It says, "His name is J-O-H-N."

Elizabeth laughs and holds the baby close. "John," she whispers in her son's tiny ear.

Suddenly, Elizabeth hears a familiar voice. "Praise the Lord, the God of Israel!" it says. It is Zechariah. He can speak again!

Everyone is amazed to hear Zechariah's voice. "This is incredible!" they say. "Who will this child turn out to be?"

Zechariah takes his baby boy in his arms. God's Spirit fills him, showing him the future. "You, my little son, will be called the prophet of the Most High," he says. "You will prepare the way for the Lord and tell his people how to find salvation."

To learn more about the birth of John the Baptist, read Luke 1:39-80.

The bus pulls away from Zechariah and Elizabeth's home and continues down the road. Soon some travelers appear in the distance. "I think I see Mary up ahead," Griffin says, squinting out the front window.

"Where?" Munch asks. Griffin points to a woman riding on a donkey.

"It is Mary!" Munch exclaims.

"Griffin, are we traveling toward Bethlehem?" Lana asks.

Griffin takes a peek at the map. "Yep."

"This is it!" Lana squeals. "We got to see John the Baptist as a baby, and now we're going to see the newborn baby Jesus!"

Mary shifts from side to side on the donkey's saddle, trying to get comfortable. She is tired and sore after the long journey from Nazareth to Bethlehem. The Roman emperor had ordered all of his subjects to go to their hometowns so that he could count them all. Joseph's family is from Bethlehem, so even though Mary will have her baby very soon, they started out on their trip.

When Mary and Joseph reach Bethlehem, they are exhausted. "Please find us a place to rest," Mary begs Joseph. Joseph knocks on door after door, but he gets the same answer again and again. "We don't have room. Try somewhere else." No one has a place for Mary and Joseph to stay.

Joseph gets desperate. He knocks on more doors. Still, there is no room. Ready to give up, he approaches one last door. "My house is already full of travelers," says the man who opens the door. Joseph turns away sadly, putting his arm around Mary, who is trying not to cry. "Wait," says the man. "You can stay in my stable if you want. It's

BUILD YOUR FAITH!

The angel told the shepherds that the Savior had been born. Earlier, the angel that appeared to Joseph in his dream told him that Mary "will have a son, and you are to name him Jesus, for he will save his people from their sins" (Matthew 1:21). Jesus came to be our Savior and to take away our sins in order to *save* us from being separated from God forever. Have you asked him to save you from your sins? If not, or if you're not sure what it all means, ask a parent, pastor, or other trusted adult to talk to you about it. It's the most important decision you could ever make!

nothing fancy, but it's all I can offer you." The man shows Mary and Joseph the stable.

Joseph looks into the stable at all the animals, then back at Mary. She goes right inside. "This will do for the night," she says. Joseph thanks the man and follows Mary into the stable.

Mary and Joseph go to sleep listening to the sounds of cows, sheep, and goats. Their donkey munches hay loudly, happy to be done with the long journey.

In the middle of the night, Mary wakes up suddenly. She sits up, then stands and walks around a little. After a while, she wakes Joseph. "It's time," she tells him.

"Time for what?" Joseph asks. Mary points at her huge stomach. "Right now?" Joseph asks, looking around at the animals.

"Yes! Right now!" Mary says.

After many hours, Mary gives birth to a baby boy. She wraps her baby in strips of cloth and lays him in a manger, or feed box. "Look at how beautiful he is," Mary says to Joseph.

Joseph touches the baby's tiny cheek. "Baby Jesus," he says softly. "The Son of God."

That night, in the fields outside Bethlehem, a group of shepherds watch over their sheep. The sheep sleep huddled together, quiet except for a *baa* here and there. The shepherds stretch out near the fire. A few of them talk softly to one another. Some of them are nodding off to sleep.

Suddenly, the brightest light the shepherds and sheep have ever seen shines all around them. Then an angel appears! Some of the shepherds are frozen with panic, while others dive for cover. The sheep run around in a frenzy.

"Don't be afraid!" the angel says. "I have wonderful news! The Savior is born today in Bethlehem. Go and see him. Look for a baby wrapped in strips of cloth and sleeping in a manger."

Then, the angel is joined by an entire army of angels! They praise God, saying, "Glory to God in highest heaven, and peace to the people who please God!" Then they disappear, and the night is dark and quiet once again.

The shepherds stare at each other for a long time. Then one of them says, "Well, let's go! Let's go find the Savior." The shepherds travel to Bethlehem and find the stable where Mary, Joseph, and baby Jesus are resting. The shepherds fall on their knees in front of the manger and worship the Son of God.

To learn more about the birth of Jesus, read Luke 2:1-20.

A Visit to the Temple

"Spinning sprockets! I can't believe we just saw the first Christmas!" Munch says.

"It was amazing!" Lana agrees. "Where to next?" she asks Griffin.

Griffin unfolds his map. "Bethlehem is really close to Jerusalem," he says. "Looks like we are headed back there." Lana, Griffin, and Munch watch out the window as the walls of Jerusalem come into view.

Mary and Joseph climb the magnificent steps that lead to the Temple. They have traveled from Bethlehem to Jerusalem with their newborn son. The law of Moses says that Jewish parents must present their firstborn son at the Temple, make an offering, and dedicate the baby's life to the Lord. Mary and Joseph are obeying the law by bringing Jesus to the Temple. Joseph carries two pigeons in a cage for their offering.

Just inside the Temple doors, Mary stops to make sure the baby's blanket is wrapped tightly around him. An old man watches her from a distance. The man's name is Simeon, and he has been listening to and obeying God for a long time. Simeon has been waiting years for this moment. The Holy Spirit told Simeon that he would not die until he saw the Messiah, the promised rescuer of the Jewish people, with his very own eyes.

As soon as he sees Jesus, Simeon recognizes that this baby is the Messiah. He walks over to Mary and Joseph. "May I?" he asks, holding out his arms. Mary looks into the old man's kind eyes and hands baby Jesus to Simeon. "Oh, how I have longed for this moment!" Simeon says, holding baby Jesus close to his chest. "Praise God!" Tears of joy run down the old man's cheeks.

Simeon turns to Mary and says, "This child will cause many to fall in Israel, but he will bring such joy to others. God sent Jesus, yet many will be against him."

An old woman named Anna overhears what Simeon says. Anna is nearly always at the Temple and spends almost all of her time praying and worshiping God. She comes to look at baby Jesus. "Praise God!" she cries. Anna can't wait to tell everyone she sees about the newborn Savior, the Messiah.

To learn more about Simeon, Anna, and Jesus' dedication, read Luke 2:21-38.

"Whoa, look at that palace!" Munch says, pointing ahead. "And check out those guys in the fancy clothes!"

"I think those are the wise men," Lana says. "This must be Herod's palace."

The wise men enter the palace. Looking around at the beautiful furniture and decorations, they wonder if this is the place. The wise men have traveled a very long way. They are searching for a baby, but not just any baby. They are searching for a newborn king.

The wise men are brought to King Herod. "I have heard that you are looking for a king," Herod says, glaring at them. "I am the only king around here."

"We are looking for a baby king," one of the wise men says. "We saw his star as it rose, and we have come to worship him."

"A baby whose birth is marked by such a beautiful star will become a very important king," says another wise man.

King Herod scowls. Sometimes people call him "Herod the Great," which he loves, but Herod is not a great man at all. He is evil and will do anything to stay in power. He is terribly jealous at the thought of a new king. *This baby might replace me,* he thinks. He comes up with a sneaky and horrible plan.

"It's your lucky day," King Herod tells the wise men. "It's a good thing you came to me. When I heard that you were in town, looking for a new king, I called a meeting of religious leaders and asked them where a Jewish king called the Messiah would be born. I thought that the baby you are looking for must surely be this Messiah. The religious leaders told me that the prophets said that the Messiah would be born in Bethlehem. So go to Bethlehem and find the baby Messiah. Then come back here and tell me where he is, so I can worship him too."

THINK ABOUT IT!

[The wise men] entered the house and saw the child with his mother, Mary, and they bowed down and worshiped him. Then they opened their treasure chests and gave him gifts of gold, frankincense, and myrrh.

Matthew 2:11

The wise men gave Jesus very valuable gifts to show that they knew he was a great king. Gold is something that we still consider valuable today. Frankincense and myrrh are both resins, a substance that comes from certain kinds of trees. The trees that produce frankincense and myrrh grow in Africa, India, and the Arabian Peninsula. Frankincense and myrrh give off a strong smell that many people like. They were used for perfume, in religious ceremonies, and even as medicine in ancient times. Some people think that these expensive gifts may have provided the money that Joseph, Mary, and Jesus needed to escape to Egypt.

SLOW!

But Herod does not really want to worship the new baby king. He wants to kill the child instead.

"Thank you, King Herod!" the wise men say. "We will go to Bethlehem right away."

The wise men hurry out of Herod's palace. It has gotten dark while they were speaking to the king. "Look!" one of them says, pointing to the sky. The star they saw in their homeland is shining brightly, showing them where to go. The wise men follow the star to Bethlehem, where they find a small house. "We're here! This is the place!" the wise men say, filled with joy. They enter the house and see Jesus with Mary. The wise men bow down and worship the little king. Then they give Jesus rich and expensive gifts—gold, frankincense, and myrrh.

"Do not go back the same way you came," God warns the wise men when it is time to leave. "King Herod wishes to harm Jesus." So the wise men go home by a different route.

To learn more about the visit of the wise men, read Matthew 2:1-12.

A Midnight Trip to Egypt

After the wise men leave, Mary and Joseph tuck Jesus into bed. The two parents talk about their exciting day, the mysterious strangers, and the beautiful gifts Jesus received. Then they also get in bed for a good night's rest.

An angel appears to Joseph in his dream. "Get up, Joseph!" the angel says. "You must take Mary and Jesus to Egypt right away! Soon Herod will come looking for the child to kill him."

Joseph wakes up with a start. He knows that was no ordinary dream. He shakes Mary gently. "Wake up," he whispers to her. "We need to leave."

"Leave?" Mary is sleepy and confused. "Where are we going?"

"Egypt," Joseph tells her. "God has warned me that King Herod will try to kill Jesus. We must escape before he finds us."

Mary gasps and runs to get Jesus while Joseph packs up some of their things. While it is still dark, the family slips out of Bethlehem, walking down the road that will eventually take them to Egypt.

To learn more about the escape to Egypt, read Matthew 2:13-18.

A Mad Dash through Jerusalem

"I'm glad they got away!" Munch says to Lana. She nods.

Looking in the Bible, Lana says, "Mary, Joseph, and Jesus stay in Egypt until King Herod dies. Then they move back to Nazareth. The next story about Jesus in the Bible talks about a trip he makes to Jerusalem with Mary and Joseph when he's about 12 years old."

"Jerusalem! That's where we're going next," Griffin says.

Mary and Joseph have been running up and down the streets of Jerusalem all day, frantically searching for their son. "Jesus! Jesus!" Mary calls out for the thousandth time. "Oh, Joseph, we have to find him!" she cries. Joseph squeezes her hand. "Jesus!" Mary calls again. But there is no answer. Mary and Joseph have looked in the marketplace. They have searched every backstreet and alley in Jerusalem. Jesus is nowhere to be found.

Exhausted and discouraged, Mary sinks down onto a bench. "I can't believe it took us a whole day to realize that Jesus wasn't with us!" she says, wiping at a tear running down her face. Mary and Joseph travel to Jerusalem for the Passover every year, and this year they brought Jesus with them for the first time. He is 12 years old, almost old enough to join the synagogue, where Jewish people gather to worship God. They always go with a large group of friends and relatives, so Mary and Joseph weren't concerned that they didn't see Jesus on their way out of Jerusalem after the Passover celebration. But when he didn't show up for dinner that night, they started to worry. After a full day traveling back to Jerusalem and another day of searching, it has been three days since Mary has seen her boy.

"Where can he be?" Mary asks Joseph. "Where have we not looked?"

Joseph glances at the setting sun. Soon it will be dark, and they will have to stop searching for the night. He looks at Mary's frightened face. "Let's go back to the Temple," Joseph says. "Then we'll retrace our steps out of Jerusalem. We'll ask everyone we can find if they've seen Jesus."

The tired and worried parents go back to the Temple. They stop a Temple worker and ask him if he has seen a 12-year-old boy recently.

"Oh, yes," the Temple worker says. "There has been a young man here talking with the teachers for the past few days. The teachers are amazed at how much the boy knows about God's Word."

The Temple worker leads Mary and Joseph to where a group of religious teachers is gathered. A young boy is sitting and talking with them. It's Jesus!

Mary rushes up to her son and grabs him tightly. She starts to cry. "Why did you do this to us?" she says, shaking and squeezing Jesus. "Your father and I have been worried sick."

Jesus smiles at his mother and wipes away her tears. "Why were you worried?" he asks her. "Didn't you know that I would be in my Father's house?"

Mary and Joseph are puzzled by Jesus' words, but mostly they are happy and relieved to have found him. The family travels home to Nazareth together. Jesus is an obedient son, and he grows up strong and wise. And Mary sometimes sits quietly and thinks about all the wonderful and strange things that have happened.

To learn more about Jesus in the Temple, read Luke 2:41-52.

Down to the River

The bus leaves Jerusalem and heads toward the Jordan River. Soon the kids can see a man standing in the middle of the rushing water. "Who's that?" Munch asks, pointing to a strange-looking man.

"That's John, Zechariah and Elizabeth's son," Lana says. "Some people call him John the Baptist now."

"That's the little baby we saw? He's all grown up now!" Munch says. "What is he eating?"

Munch cringes as John, who's moved to the shore, takes a locust, dips it in honey, and places it in his mouth.

Crunch! John chews the insect ferociously. He wipes a few crumbs off his clothes, which are made of camel hair, and wades back into the Jordan River. There is a long line of people waiting to be baptized by John in the river. They want John to dunk them in the water to show they will stop sinning and live a life that is pleasing to God. John tells everyone about God's Kingdom. "Turn to God," John says. "The Kingdom of Heaven is near!"

John leans down and washes his hands in the river. The water flows gently around his waist. Then he calls each person, one by one, into the river and baptizes him or her.

Repent of your sins and turn to God, for the Kingdom of Heaven is near.

Matthew 3:2

PARK HERE!

READ AND MEMORIZE THIS VERSE.

"There is someone coming who is greater than me," John tells the people. "I am not good enough to be his slave. I baptize you with water, but he will baptize you with the Holy Spirit."

The crowd listens carefully. "Who is he talking about?" they wonder.

One day Jesus stands in the crowd, listening to John. Stepping forward, he asks, "Will you baptize me next?"

John knows that Jesus is the one he has been telling everyone about. "You should be the one baptizing me," John tells Jesus.

"God wants you to do this," Jesus says, smiling. So John agrees.

Jesus enters the Jordan River, and John dunks him under the water. When Jesus comes back up, the heavens open and the Holy Spirit comes down. The Spirit looks like a dove that lands on Jesus. John hears a loud voice from heaven say, "This is my dear Son, who makes me very happy."

To learn more about Jesus' baptism,
read Matthew 3:1-17;
Mark 1:1-11;
Luke 3:1-22;
John 1:19-34.

Water to Wine

The bus leaves the Jordan River, heading northwest. After a while, it reaches a town. The sign outside the bus window reads "Cana."

"Look!" Lana says. "Someone is having a party." Lana, Griffin, and Munch watch the celebration through the bus window.

"I think it's a wedding," Griffin says. "There are the bride and groom."

CANA

- Cana was a town in Galilee that is located not far from Nazareth. Its name means "place of reeds."
- Cana is the place where Jesus performed his first miracle—turning water into wine at a wedding celebration.
- Nathanael, one of Jesus' disciples, was from Cana.

Fun Fact: Scholars do not agree on the exact location of Cana. Five different spots are considered to be possibilities for where it may have been.

The bride's smile shines even brighter than all her jewelry. The groom laughs with his friends and beams with pride every time he glances over at his new wife. All the guests are enjoying themselves, eating, drinking, talking, and dancing.

But the servants frown and whisper to each other. "What are we supposed to serve the guests?" one of them asks another. "We are out of wine."

"This is so embarrassing!" the other servant moans.

Mary is sitting nearby, chatting with a few friends. She overhears the servants' whispers and she frowns. Running out of wine in the middle of a wedding celebration will be very embarrassing for the groom's family. The guests will consider it an insult, and the whole town will talk about it for years. Mary looks around for her oldest son. She knows that if anyone can help, Jesus can.

Jesus is just sitting down from dancing, laughing and out of breath. He smiles at Mary as she walks up to him. "Son," Mary says, "the hosts are nearly out of wine. Is there anything you can do?"

"Dear mother," Jesus says. "My time has not yet come."

Like many times before, Mary isn't sure what Jesus means, but she

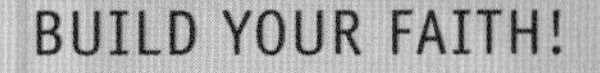

BUILD YOUR FAITH!

When Mary noticed a problem at the wedding, she went to Jesus and asked for his help. Even though she didn't understand his answer and didn't know what he was going to do to help, she trusted him to do the right thing. When you have a problem, do you turn to Jesus? Do you trust that he will do what's best for you, even if you don't understand it?

UNDER CONSTRUCTION!

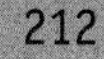

goes over to the servants who are clustered anxiously in the doorway. She points to Jesus. "Do whatever that man tells you," she says.

Then Jesus comes over. He points to six huge water jars that stand nearby. "Fill those jars to the top with water," he tells the servants. They fill the jars and look to Jesus for more instructions. "Dip some out, and take it to the master of ceremonies," Jesus says.

The servants pour a drink from one of the jars. They are shocked to see that what comes out of the jar isn't water, but a deep, rich wine! They take it to the master of ceremonies, who tastes it. "This is delicious!" he says. He calls the groom over. "I've never heard of such a thing," the master of ceremonies says to the groom. "Usually hosts serve their best wine first, but you saved the best for last!"

The servants pour wine for the guests, and the party continues. Jesus' mother and some of his friends realize that Jesus changed the water into wine. They are amazed at his power and believe he is the Son of God.

To learn more about how Jesus turned water into wine, read John 2:1-12.

A Late-Night Visit

The bus drives south, back toward Jerusalem. Night has fallen by the time the children enter the city. A man comes down the street, walking quickly and quietly, as if he doesn't want to be seen.

"What's that guy up to?" Munch asks.

The man is a highly respected Jewish religious leader named Nicodemus. Nicodemus picks up his pace and pulls his hood over his head. He doesn't want the other religious leaders in the city to know what he is doing. Nicodemus is on his way to visit Jesus. He has heard many stories about Jesus, and he wonders if they are true. He wants to see Jesus and decide for himself who this man really is.

Looking left, then right, Nicodemus crosses the street and enters the place where Jesus is waiting. Nicodemus and Jesus sit down together to talk.

"Jesus, we all know that God is with you and that he has sent you to teach us," Nicodemus says.

Jesus replies, "Unless you are born again, you cannot see the Kingdom of God."

"I don't understand what you mean," Nicodemus says. "How can a man be born twice?"

"Humans give birth to human babies, but the Holy Spirit gives birth to spiritual life," Jesus explains. "Just like you can hear the wind, but you can't tell where it comes from or where it's going, so you can't explain how someone is born of the Spirit."

Nicodemus leans forward in his seat. "How is this possible?" he asks.

"You are an important Jewish teacher, and you don't understand?" Jesus says. "If you don't believe me when I tell you about earthly things, how will you believe me when I tell you about heavenly things?"

Nicodemus scratches his head. He is very confused.

"No one has ever gone to heaven and come back to earth," Jesus continues. "But the Son of Man has come down from heaven. God loved the world so much that he sent his only Son to save everyone who believes in him."

Nicodemus gets up. It's been a confusing visit, and now he must return home. *Jesus has definitely given me a lot to think about,* he thinks as he scurries back down the street.

This is how God loved the world: He gave his one and only Son, so that everyone who believes in him will not perish but have eternal life.

John 3:16

PARK HERE!

READ AND MEMORIZE THIS VERSE.

To learn more about Nicodemus visiting Jesus, read John 3:1-21.

Follow the Leader

The bus drives along the Jordan River until it reaches a huge freshwater lake. "How beautiful!" Lana says, watching the sun sparkle on the water. "Look at the boats!"

"I think those guys are fishing," Munch says. "It looks like fun."

"This is the Sea of Galilee," Griffin says.

Jesus stands on the shore of the sea, preaching to a group of people. They are so eager to hear what he is saying that they press closer and closer, crowding Jesus. He notices two empty fishing boats on the shore. The owners of the boats are cleaning their nets nearby. Jesus climbs into one of the boats and waves to its owner, a fisherman named Peter. Peter comes over and pushes the boat into the water, and Jesus speaks to the people from the boat. The boat rocks gently from side to side as Jesus sits in it.

GALILEE/SEA OF GALILEE

- Galilee was a region in northern Israel.
- Some physical features in Galilee include lakes, streams, a river, mountains, and forests.
- Jesus did most of his teaching and miracles in Galilee.
- The Sea of Galilee is a large freshwater lake. Many people in Galilee fished for a living.
- Galilee has many mountains. The Sermon on the Mount took place on a mountain overlooking the Sea of Galilee.
- The climate in Galilee is warm and was good for growing crops. Winters are mild. Near the Sea of Galilee, it is more tropical.
- Galileans grew wheat, olives, figs, dates, and other vegetables. They only ate meat on special occasions, though many who lived near the Sea of Galilee ate fish.
- The largest fishing village on the shore of the Sea of Galilee was called Capernaum. Jesus used Capernaum as his home base when he taught and did miracles in Galilee.

Fun Fact: The first four disciples that Jesus called were living in Galilee.

When Jesus is done speaking, he turns to Peter and his brother, Andrew. "Go out into the deep water," Jesus tells them. "Let's do some fishing."

Peter and Andrew look at each other. They have met Jesus before, when Andrew was a follower of John the Baptist. They know that he is no ordinary man. "Master," Peter says, "we tried to fish all night, but our nets came up empty. But if you want to, we can try again." Jesus nods. Peter, Andrew, and Jesus sail into deeper water.

Reaching their destination, Peter and Andrew lower their nets. They watch as the nets sink into the water, then after a while, they pull on ropes to bring them back up. It is much harder than Peter and Andrew expected. They have to pull with all their might. When they bring the nets up to the surface, the nets are overflowing with fish!

Peter and Andrew have trouble getting the heavy nets into the boat. They shout for their partners, James and John, to grab a boat and come help them. Together, they all tug on the heavy nets, pulling them out of the water and into the boats. Soon, both boats are so full of fish that they almost sink. The fishermen can't believe their eyes!

Peter kneels before Jesus, bowing his head. "Oh, Lord, please go away!" he says. "I am too much of a sinner to be around you." Andrew, James, and John stare at Jesus in awe.

Jesus smiles at the fishermen. "Don't be afraid!" he says. "Come and follow me. I will teach you how to fish for people!"

As soon as the boats reach the shore,

THINK ABOUT IT!

One day as Jesus was walking along the shore of the Sea of Galilee, he saw two brothers—Simon, also called Peter, and Andrew—throwing a net into the water, for they fished for a living.

Matthew 4:18

The Sea of Galilee is really a large lake. Many people fished on it in Jesus' time; there were 30 fishing towns on the shores of the lake. In those days, many fishermen used bell-shaped nets with weights tied to the edges. They would throw the nets onto the water, where the nets would sink, trapping fish under them. Then the fishermen would pull on a rope to close the net and keep the fish inside.

SLOW!

Peter, Andrew, James, and John drop everything and immediately follow Jesus. They leave behind their boats, their nets full with fish, and their families. They know that following Jesus is the most important thing they can do.

Early one morning, Jesus calls all of his followers together. "I am going to choose 12 of you to be my special helpers," he says. He starts calling out names. "Peter. Andrew. James. John." The four fishermen rush to Jesus' side. "Philip. Nathanael. Matthew." Some of Jesus' followers whisper among themselves. Matthew used to be a tax collector, and many people think he is greedy and dishonest. "Thomas. James, son of Alphaeus. Simon." Even more people whisper. Simon used to be a rebel soldier, fighting against the Roman government. "Thaddaeus. And Judas." Jesus' 12 helpers, called disciples or apostles, come from different backgrounds and have different jobs. None of the men are perfect, but they all are eager to learn from Jesus.

To learn more about Jesus' disciples, read Matthew 4:18-22; 9:9-13; Mark 1:16-20; 2:13-17; 3:13-19; Luke 5:1-11, 27-32; 6:12-16; John 1:35-51.

Called Back to Life

The bus drives a bit farther down the rocky beach and then cuts its engine. "Why are we stopping?" Griffin asks.

"I'm not sure," Lana says.

"Well, as long as the bus is parked, I'm going to rest," Griffin says. He closes his eyes for a few minutes. When he opens them, Griffin is amazed to see the shore lined with people of all ages. He notices that some of the people are blind, sick, or limping. Puzzled, he sits up in his seat to get a better view.

The crowd on the shore continues to grow. They are waiting for Jesus to arrive in a boat. Many of the people are hurt or sick. They hope Jesus can heal them.

As soon as Jesus steps off the boat, people rush toward him. A lot of commotion comes from the back of the crowd. A man is pushing and shoving people left and right, trying desperately to get to Jesus.

"Please let me through!" he shouts. "My little girl is very sick! She's dying! I need to see Jesus!"

The man's name is Jairus, and he is an important man—the leader of the synagogue. The desperate father reaches Jesus. He falls down at Jesus' feet and begs for help. "My daughter is dying!" he cries. "Please come touch her and heal her."

"I will come," Jesus says. He and his disciples follow as Jairus runs toward his home. All the people follow too. No one wants to leave Jesus' side.

A woman makes her way through the crowd. She is too shy to push, but every time she sees the tiniest space between two people, she slips into it. The woman has been sick for 12 years. She has given all her money to doctors, but they have made her worse instead of better. Jesus is her only hope. *If I can just touch Jesus' clothes, I will be healed,* the woman thinks to herself as she squeezes through the crowd. *I know he is that powerful.* Finally, she is right behind Jesus. She stretches out her hand as far as she can. Her fingers barely brush the hem of Jesus' robe. Suddenly, the woman knows she has been healed! She feels better than she ever has in her whole life.

The woman tries to hide in the crowd, but Jesus turns around. "Who touched me?" he asks, looking around at the people.

"It wasn't me," someone says.

"Me either," says someone else. Everyone shakes their heads while the healed woman tries to hide behind a tall man.

Jesus' disciples look puzzled. "Master," Peter says, "who isn't touching you? This whole crowd has been pressing up against you ever since we got off the boat."

"Someone touched my robe on purpose," Jesus insists. "I felt healing power go out from me."

The woman realizes that there is no escaping Jesus. Shaking with fear, she walks up to him and falls to her knees. Everyone is silent as she explains to Jesus why she touched him.

Jesus smiles at her, takes

her hand, and lifts her to her feet. "Daughter," he says, "your faith has made you well."

Everyone smiles. But then they hear a terrible cry. "We're too late!" Jairus wails. A messenger from home has brought him awful news. "My daughter is dead!"

Jesus puts his arm around Jairus. "Don't be afraid," he tells the sobbing father. "Just have faith, and your daughter will be healed." Jairus looks up at Jesus with hope. He leads Jesus to his house. Jesus tells everyone except Peter, James, and John to wait outside.

The house is filled with crying people. Jairus's wife runs to her husband, sobbing.

"Why are you all crying?" Jesus asks. "This little girl isn't dead; she's only sleeping."

The people laugh at Jesus and shake their heads in disbelief. "She is definitely dead," they say.

Jesus sends everyone except for his three followers and the girl's parents out of the house. They go into the little girl's room, where she is lying on her bed. Jesus takes the girl's hand and bends down to speak in her ear. "Little girl, get up!" he says. The girl immediately opens her eyes and stands up. Everyone in the room is shocked. The girl's parents run to her and throw their arms around her, their tears of sadness turning into tears of joy.

To learn more about how Jesus brought the little girl back to life, read Matthew 9:18-26; Mark 5:21-43; Luke 8:40-56.

A Picnic for 5,000

"It's time for a picnic!" Lana says, closing the Bible.

"Really? I'm starved!" Munch says.

"Not for us!" Lana laughs. "The picnic is for all of Jesus' followers!"

Griffin studies the map while the bus drives far out into the country. "We're still in the region of Galilee," he says without looking up.

"It looks like the middle of nowhere to me," Munch says. "But I can still see the sea."

The sun is hot, shining down from a cloudless sky. Sweat dampens the heads of men, women, and children as they wait. They have walked for a long time to get here. They look out over the Sea of Galilee, waiting. Finally someone shouts, "There he is!"

A boat appears on the horizon. Jesus and his followers are on it. They have come to this spot, far away from the towns, so that they can rest and be alone. Jesus has been so busy teaching and healing people that he and his friends haven't even had time to eat regular meals. But the people figured out where Jesus was going and beat him here.

When Jesus' disciples see the people waiting for them on the shore, they sigh loudly. But Jesus smiles at the people. He welcomes them and heals them all day long. In the late afternoon, some of Jesus' friends come up to him. "It's getting late, and we're out here in the middle of nowhere," they say. "You had better send these people away so they can go buy something for dinner."

"Oh, that's all right," Jesus says. "You can feed them."

Jesus' disciples glance at each other. "Philip," Jesus says, "where can we buy food for all these people?"

"There are 5,000 men here—not even counting the women and children!" Philip says. "We would have to work for months to make enough money to buy food for them all!"

BUILD YOUR FAITH!

Jesus' followers knew that there was no way they could find enough food for more than 5,000 people to eat. It was an impossible situation! But they gathered the food they could find and followed Jesus' instructions. And God did a miracle and fed the people! Are you facing a situation that seems impossible? Do what you can, and obey what God says in his Word. Then trust God to take care of the rest.

Andrew steps forward. He is holding the hand of a little boy who has five loaves of bread and two fish in a small basket. "This is the only food I could find," Andrew says.

"Thank you," says Jesus. "This will be enough. Tell the people to sit down." Jesus thanks his Father for the food and starts breaking off pieces of bread and fish. He hands the food to his friends, telling them to pass it out to the seated men, women, and children. They don't understand how such a small amount of food will feed such a large crowd. But they do as Jesus commands. Andrew hands out all the food he is carrying and goes back to Jesus to get more. Jesus fills his arms with bread and fish again. And again. And again. The same thing happens for the rest of Jesus' followers.

Stories Jesus Told

Jesus often taught with stories, called parables. He used common word pictures and situations from the time and place he lived in to explain what God and his Kingdom are like.

God is like . . .

a farmer planting seeds
(Matthew 13:1-9, 24-30; Mark 4:1-9, 26-29; Luke 8:4-8)

a king who forgives an enormous debt
(Matthew 18:21-35)

a shepherd searching for his lost sheep
(Matthew 18:12-14; Luke 15:1-7)

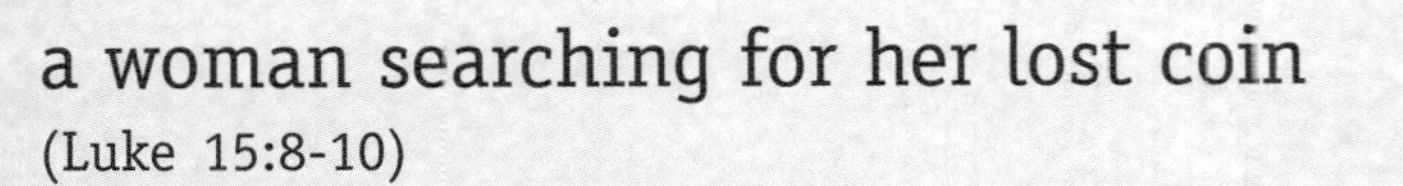

a woman searching for her lost coin
(Luke 15:8-10)

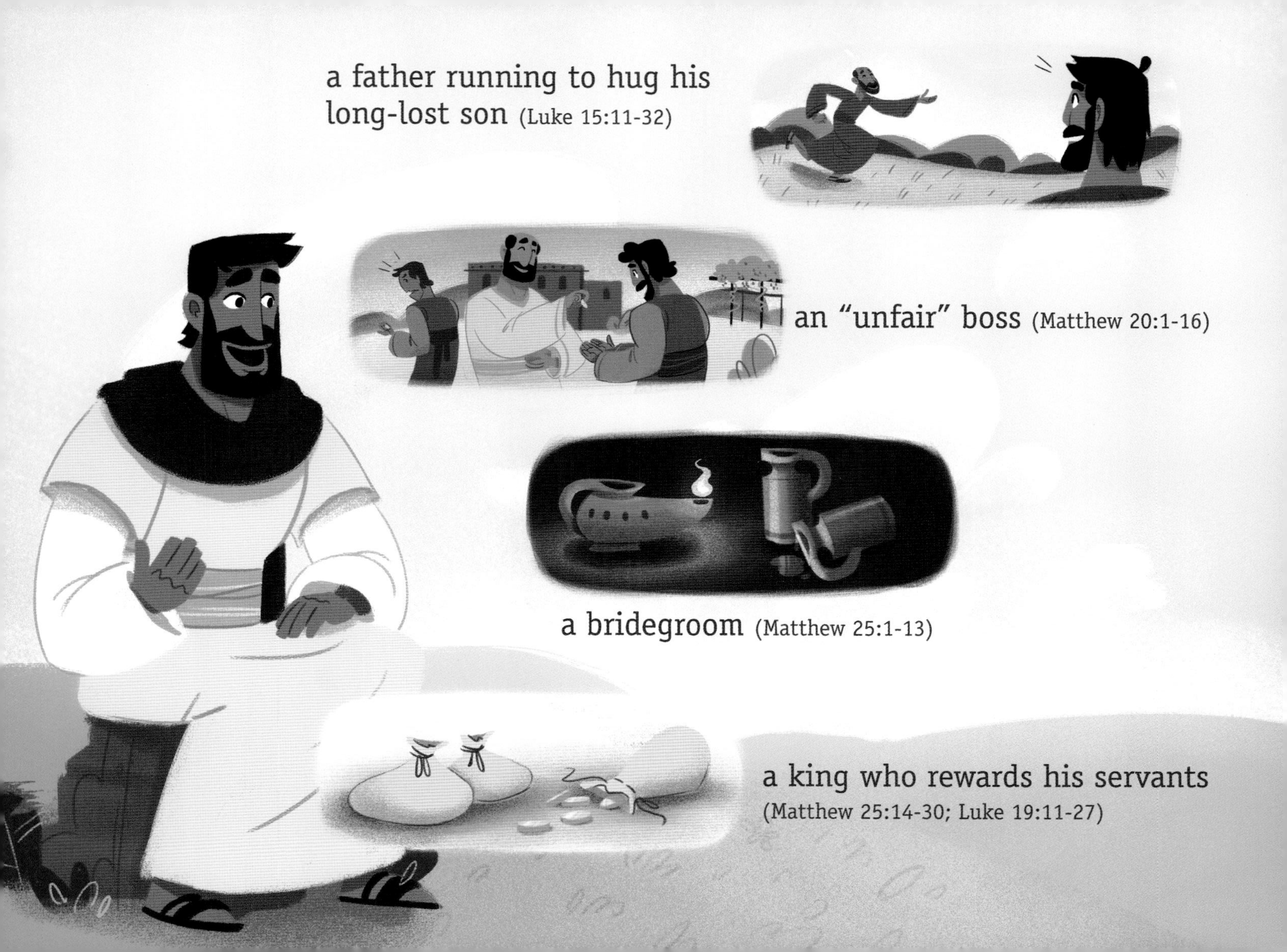

a father running to hug his long-lost son (Luke 15:11-32)

an "unfair" boss (Matthew 20:1-16)

a bridegroom (Matthew 25:1-13)

a king who rewards his servants (Matthew 25:14-30; Luke 19:11-27)

Finally everyone is eating happily. There is enough for Jesus and his friends, too! "At last, we get to sit down and eat a meal!" Peter says. Jesus smiles at the huge picnic on the hillside.

When everyone has finished eating, Jesus tells his followers to go and gather the leftovers. "We don't want to waste anything," he says.

Jesus' friends each take a basket and go to collect the extra food. When they come back, Philip inspects the baskets. All 12 of them are full. "Jesus has turned a few fish and loaves of bread into enough food to feed thousands!" he says to himself. He is amazed at Jesus' power.

To learn more about Jesus feeding 5,000 people, read Matthew 14:13-21; Mark 6:30-44; Luke 9:10-17; John 6:1-15.

An Unusual Way to Travel by Sea

The bus drives back toward the Sea of Galilee. The sky turns black, and wind pounds the side of the bus. Then rain begins to pour down.

"This is a bad storm," Griffin says. "But at least we're safe on the bus. I wouldn't want to be that little boat out there!" Griffin points to the sea, where a tiny boat is bobbing around on the huge waves.

"That's the disciples' boat!" Lana says.

Jesus' disciples are tossed around in their little boat out on the Sea of Galilee. Andrew, Peter, James, and John hold the oars, rowing as hard as they can. Nathanael, Philip, Simon, and the other James are ready to take over when someone gets too tired to row. Matthew, Thomas, Thaddaeus, and Judas use buckets to bail water out of the boat. They are all exhausted and frightened. *If only Jesus were with us!* they all think. Jesus had sent them ahead while he said good-bye to the crowds after the big picnic. He wanted some time alone to pray. Jesus' friends were happy to give him some time to himself. But now they are in big trouble.

Jesus can see them from the shore. He shields his eyes against the rain and wind as he looks over the waves at the struggling boat. Then Jesus steps onto the water. He walks on top of the waves!

Thomas is dumping a bucketful of water over the side of the boat when he sees Jesus walking toward him. He screams in terror. "A ghost!" His friends all drop what they are doing and rush over to him, making the boat lean way over onto its side. Their faces turn pale when they see Jesus.

"Don't be afraid," Jesus says. "Be brave! I am here!"

Peter swallows hard, then calls out, "Lord, if it's really you, I want to walk on the water too!"

"Come on!" Jesus says, holding out his hand.

Peter climbs over the side of the boat while his friends watch, their mouths and eyes wide and round. Peter steps onto the waves. They hold him up! Peter smiles and starts to walk toward Jesus.

But then Peter takes his eyes off Jesus and starts looking around him. He sees huge waves towering and crashing right next to him. He feels the wind, so strong that it almost knocks him down. Peter starts to feel afraid again. And then he starts to sink. "Jesus, help me!" he screams.

Right before Peter's head goes under the water, he feels someone take his hand. Jesus pulls him up out of the water. "Your faith is too small," Jesus says. "Why did you doubt me?"

Jesus and Peter walk to the boat and climb in. The wind and the waves are immediately calm. The other men are speechless. Jesus sits down in the boat, and his followers row safely to the other side of the sea. Pulling the boat ashore, they collapse in the sand.

To learn more about Jesus walking on the water, read Matthew 14:22-33; Mark 6:45-52; John 6:16-21.

Miraculous Meeting on a Mountain

"That was amazing," Griffin says. "I wish I could have walked on the water with Jesus."

Lana and Munch nod. The kids sit in silence, thinking about what they've just seen, as the bus begins to travel uphill.

"This is a tall mountain," Munch observes.

"Look, there's Jesus!" Lana says. "He's standing with three of his disciples."

Peter, James, and John hike with Jesus to the top of a high mountain to be alone and pray. "Just a little higher," Jesus says to his disciples as they climb up the rocky hillside. Peter huffs and puffs, out of breath.

When they reach the mountain's peak, Jesus kneels down in prayer. While he is speaking, something glorious happens. Right before the disciples' eyes, Jesus' appearance changes.

"Look at Jesus' face!" John cries out. "It's shining like the brightest star!"

"Look at his clothes," James whispers. "They're whiter than snow!"

"Jesus is shining brighter than any light!" Peter says.

The disciples watch Jesus with awe. Suddenly they see two men appear next to Jesus.

"That's Moses and Elijah!" John says. The disciples can't believe their eyes. Moses and Elijah both lived hundreds of years ago, but here they are, talking to Jesus!

Peter says the first thing that pops into his head. "Lord," he calls out to Jesus, "it is wonderful for us to be here! I will build three shelters to help us remember this moment. I will make the first one for you and the other two for Elijah and Moses."

THINK ABOUT IT!

Suddenly, two men, Moses and Elijah, appeared and began talking with Jesus. Luke 9:30

Moses and Elijah were considered the greatest prophets in the Old Testament. Moses represents the law—the Ten Commandments and the other rules God gave his people on Mount Sinai. Elijah represents the prophets who told God's people about the coming of the Messiah, or Savior. God sent Moses and Elijah to be with Jesus to show that Jesus was the real Messiah.

While Peter is still speaking, a bright cloud appears above the men. The disciples are terrified. A mighty voice speaks from the cloud. "This is my dear Son—my Chosen One. Listen to him." The disciples fall flat on their faces in fear.

Jesus comes over and touches them. "Get up," he says. "Don't be afraid."

When the disciples lift their heads, they see that Elijah and Moses have disappeared. Jesus is standing there alone, looking normal again.

"You must not speak of this," Jesus tells Peter, James, and John as they walk back down the mountain. "Do not tell anyone what you have seen until the Son of Man has risen from the dead." The disciples have no idea what Jesus means, but they all nod their heads in agreement.

To learn more about Jesus' Transfiguration, read Matthew 17:1-13; Mark 9:2-13; Luke 9:28-36.

Staying with Friends

The bus follows the narrow road back down the side of the mountain. Eventually, the road leads to a small village.

"Bethany." Lana reads the sign outside the window. Making right and left turns on the streets of the village, the bus finally stops in front of a small house. Inside, a woman is busy cleaning.

"Jesus will be here any minute," Martha tells her sister, Mary, as she sweeps the floor. "We have so much to do. It would be nice of you to pitch in!" Martha sweeps a cloud of dust toward her sister.

Mary doesn't respond. She's standing at the door, eagerly watching for Jesus. She's thinking of all the things she wants to ask him when he arrives.

"After I finish the floor, we'll start making dinner. It isn't every day that we have a guest like Jesus. We need to be the best hostesses ever!" Martha says. As she finishes the sweeping, Martha mentally plans all the extravagant dishes she will prepare.

Placing the broom aside, Martha busies herself in the kitchen. Soon delicious smells fill the home. Mary and Martha's brother, Lazarus, comes in, with Jesus and his disciples right behind him. Mary greets everyone and welcomes them inside. "Please, make yourselves comfortable," she says. Martha says a quick hello and gets back to preparing the bread she is making for dinner. Mary sits by Jesus' feet, on the floor that Martha has just swept.

Martha lets out a huge sigh when she sees Mary sitting down. "Look at her, acting like she's one of the disciples!" Martha grumbles to herself. Mary is listening closely to every word Jesus says.

Martha kneads the dough roughly. She even bangs it loudly on the table a few times, shooting dirty looks toward her sister. Mary is busy listening to Jesus.

An angry, bitter feeling bubbles up inside Martha. She slams the dough down and walks over to her guests. Jesus stops talking and looks up at her.

"Jesus," Martha says, "don't you think my sister should be lending me a hand in the kitchen? It's not fair that I have to do all of this work by myself! Tell her to come help me!"

Jesus smiles warmly at Martha. "Dear Martha, the details you are worried about are not important," he says. "Don't get upset about them. Mary has figured out what really matters, and it will not be taken away from her."

To learn more about Mary and Martha, read Luke 10:38-42.

Children Welcome

The bus leaves Bethany and heads down the road. This place is familiar to Griffin, Lana, and Munch by now. "The Jordan River!" they say together. The bus crosses the river.

"This region is called Perea," Griffin informs Munch and Lana.

"There he is!" a little girl shouts, pointing at Jesus from where she is riding on her father's shoulders. Jesus sits in the grass with his back resting against a tree. His eyes are closed. The girl's father and many other parents, all with

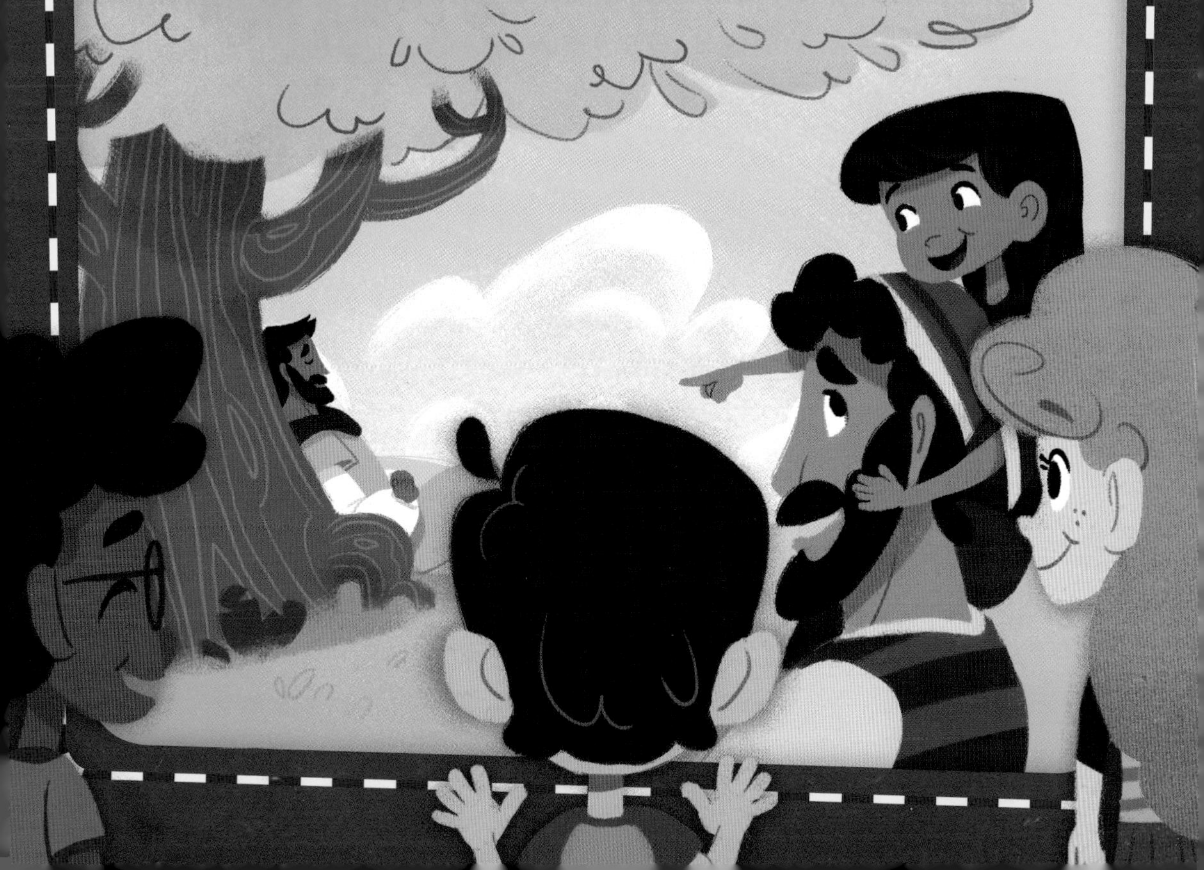

little children, flock toward Jesus. The mothers and fathers want to ask Jesus to bless their little ones.

Before the families can get to Jesus, several of his disciples come running. They hold out their hands, blocking the way. "Don't bring those children over here!" the men scold. "Our master needs to rest. Can't you see that he's tired?"

I tell you the truth, anyone who doesn't receive the Kingdom of God like a child will never enter it.
Mark 10:15

PARK HERE!
READ AND MEMORIZE THIS VERSE.

The parents and children turn away sadly. But then they hear Jesus' voice. "Let the children come to me," Jesus tells his followers. "Don't stop them! The Kingdom of God belongs to people like them." Jesus' friends move out of the way, and Jesus opens his arms. Boys and girls run through the grass to Jesus. They jump on him to give him hugs, almost knocking him over. Jesus laughs in delight. He stands and picks up a little boy, twirling him through the air. Then everyone else wants a turn.

The children's parents join the happy group, smiling and laughing, carrying the babies who are too young to walk. Jesus lays his hand on each child's head, giving every boy and girl a special blessing.

To learn more about Jesus and the children, read Matthew 19:13-15; Mark 10:13-16; Luke 18:15-17.

A Trip up a Tree

247

"We're heading west," Griffin says, looking out the window.

"How do you know?" Munch asks, rummaging in his pockets for a snack.

Griffin shrugs. "I can just tell," he says. He looks at the map. "I think we're going toward Jericho." Sure enough, the bus arrives at a large city. The sign outside the window reads "Jericho."

Munch shakes his head. "You're good," he says to Griffin.

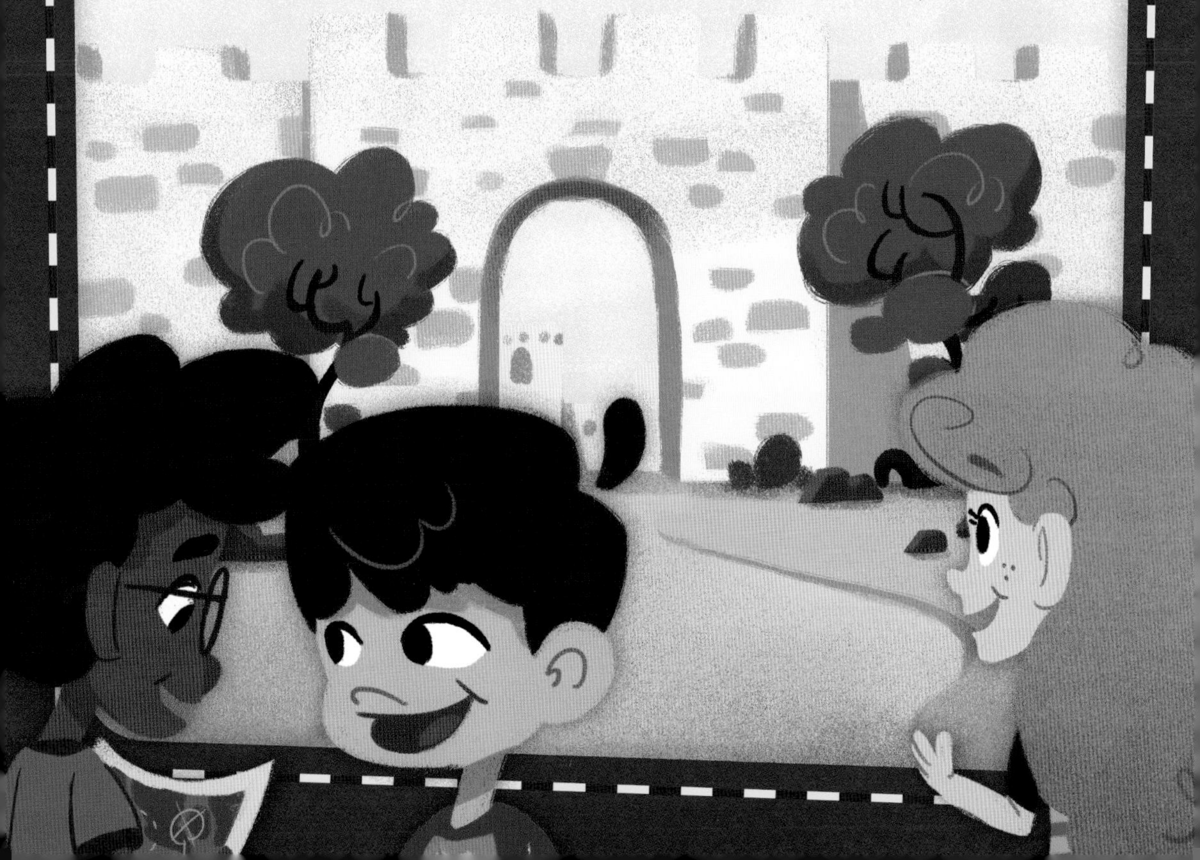

Stretching as tall as he can to grab a branch above his head, a short man hoists himself into a tree. He squirms along the branch until he's balancing just above the street. A crowd of people lines both sides of the road. They are waiting for Jesus to pass through the city of Jericho.

Noticing a shadow in front of her, a stout woman glances upward. "Is that Zacchaeus?" she asks her neighbor. "What is that scoundrel doing up there?"

The woman's friend looks up and snorts with laughter. "The great and important Zacchaeus, climbing a tree like a little boy," she giggles. "What is he thinking?"

Zacchaeus is desperate to get a good look at Jesus, but he's too short to see over the crowds of people along the road. So when he saw the sycamore-fig tree at the side of the road, he scrambled up it, not caring how silly he would look.

"Here comes Jesus!" someone calls out. The crowd falls silent as everyone strains to see the man they've heard so much about. Jesus walks down the center of the road, smiling and waving to people along the way. When he passes underneath the branch that holds Zacchaeus, he looks up.

"Hello there, Zacchaeus!" Jesus says. Zacchaeus is so surprised that he almost falls off the branch. How does Jesus know his name?

"Quick, come down from that tree!" Jesus tells Zacchaeus. "Today I will be a guest in your home." Zacchaeus climbs down as fast as he can, full of excitement and joy.

Grumbles and whispers race through the crowd. "Why would Jesus go to Zacchaeus's house?" people say to one another.

"Doesn't Jesus know Zacchaeus is a tax collector for the Romans? He is rich because he cheats people."

Jesus knows who Zacchaeus is and what he does, but he goes to Zacchaeus's home anyway. While he is there, Zacchaeus announces, "Lord, I have decided to give half of all my money to the poor. And I will pay back anyone I have cheated four times as much money as I took from them!"

Jesus smiles. "Salvation has come to this home," he says. "You truly are a son of Abraham. The Son of Man came to look for and save those who are lost."

To learn more about Jesus and Zacchaeus, read Luke 19:1-10.

A Parade for Jesus

From Jericho, the bus heads to another familiar location. "Jerusalem!" Munch says. "What are all these people doing waving leaves in the air?"

"Ooh! I bet it's the first Palm Sunday!" Lana says. "Look, there's Jesus! Riding on a donkey, just like the Bible says!" She presses her face against the window, giddy with excitement.

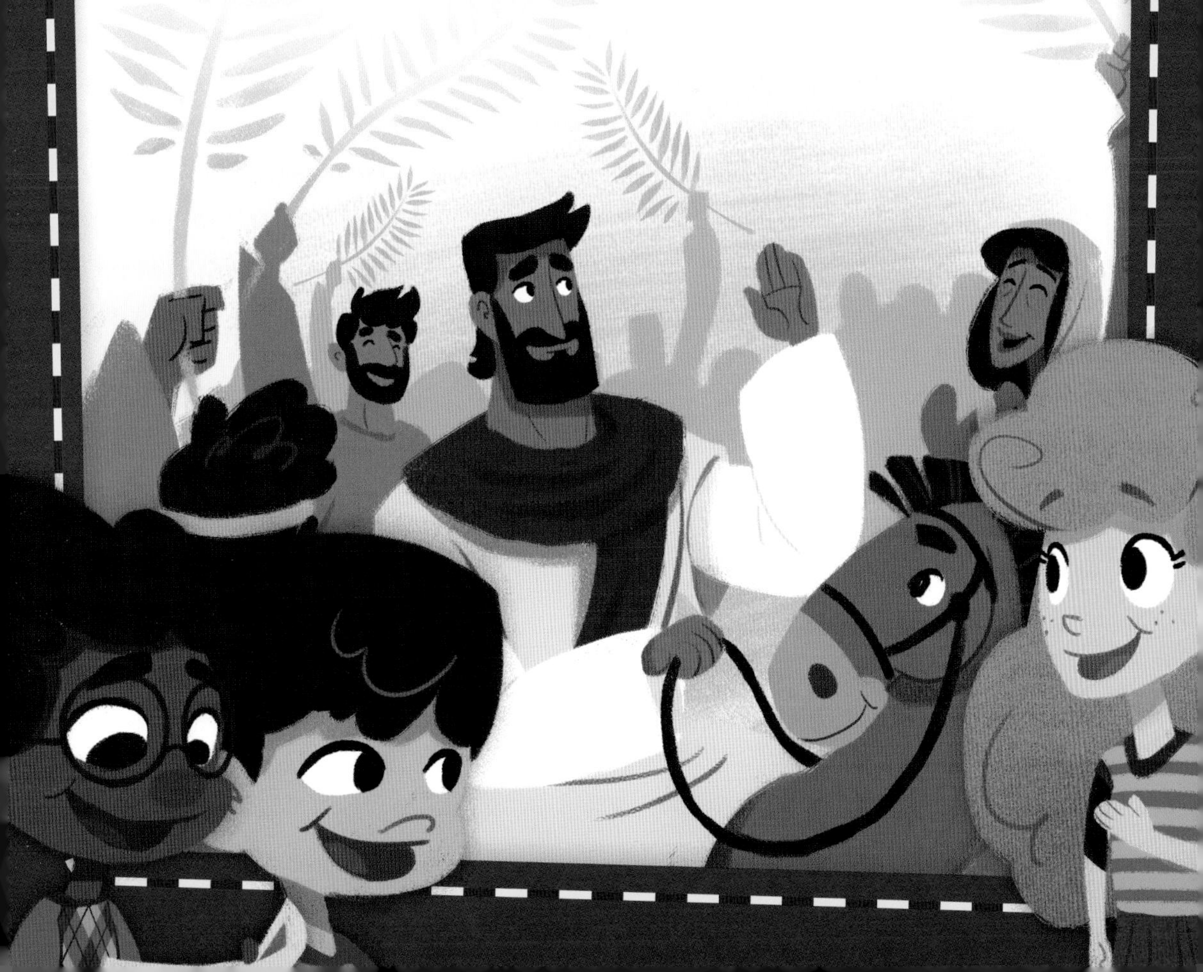

The donkey Jesus rides is so small that Jesus' feet almost brush the ground as it walks along. A short time ago, Jesus sent two of his disciples into a village near Jerusalem. "You will find a young donkey tied up there, one that no one has ever ridden," he told them. "Untie it and bring it to me." He also told them what to do if anyone tried to stop them.

The two men walked into the village and found the donkey there, just like Jesus told them. They started to untie it. "Hey!" someone shouted. "What are you doing with that donkey?"

BUILD YOUR FAITH!

As they walked into Jerusalem on the first Palm Sunday, Jesus' followers praised God for "all the wonderful miracles they had seen" (Luke 19:37). What wonderful things has God done in your life? Make a list of at least three things.

Jesus' friends answered just like Jesus told them to: "The Lord needs it," they said. "He will return it soon."

"All right," the donkey's owner said.

Now men, women, and children lay palm branches on the ground in front of Jesus as he rides into Jerusalem. The city is preparing for the Passover celebration. Jerusalem smells of delicious food. Music plays, and people dance in the streets.

Jesus' disciples walk beside him, praising God. "Hurray for the King of Israel!" all the people in the crowd shout. "Blessings on the coming Kingdom!" Someone begins to sing, and soon hundreds of voices join in.

One man lays his coat on Jesus' path.

"Blessings on the one who comes in the name of the Lord!" the man says, bowing to Jesus.

A few religious leaders watch the joyful parade, whispering angrily among themselves. "Tell the people to be quiet!" they say to Jesus. "They should not say such things."

Jesus looks the leaders in the eyes. "If my followers were quiet, the stones would start to cheer for me instead!"

To learn more about Jesus riding into Jerusalem on the first Palm Sunday, read Matthew 21:1-11; Mark 11:1-11; Luke 19:28-40; John 12:12-19.

Everyone Out!

The bus enters Jerusalem and chugs up the Temple mount. The children can see Jesus entering the Temple courtyard.

"Jesus doesn't look happy," Griffin says.

"He looks angry," Munch says.

Lana covers her face with her hands, peeking out from between her fingers.

Jesus looks around the Temple, getting angrier and angrier. He watches the merchants and listens to them calling out to customers, trying to make money on the animals being sold for sacrifices.

Jesus' face turns red, and he clenches his fists. Suddenly he walks over to one of the merchants. "How dare you?" Jesus says. He reaches under the merchant's table.

Crash! The table clatters to the ground—Jesus has flipped it over! "Everyone out!" Jesus roars. "No more using the Temple as a marketplace!"

Jesus charges from seller to seller, knocking over tables and chairs. The disciples stare with their mouths open as the merchants dive out of the way and their animals scatter, calves mooing and lambs bleating. Stacks of coins crash down from the tables of the money changers. Coins of all sizes bounce along the floor and roll into corners. Pigeons flutter around the room, adding to the commotion.

"This Temple should be a house of prayer!" Jesus shouts. "But you have turned it into a den of thieves!" The disciples watch silently. They have never seen Jesus this upset before.

When the religious leaders and teachers see the mess and hear what Jesus has done, they are furious. "We need to get rid of this so-called Messiah," they say to each other. But there is one big obstacle in the religious leaders' way—the people of Jerusalem. The people are completely amazed by Jesus and hang on every word he says.

To learn more about Jesus clearing the Temple, read Matthew 21:12-17; Mark 11:15-19; Luke 19:45-48.

A Tender Farewell

The bus leaves Jerusalem, heading down a familiar road.

"It looks like we're going back to Bethany," Griffin says.

"I hope we'll get to see Mary and Martha again," Lana says.

"Look! There they are!" Munch shouts, pointing out the window.

Mary, Martha, and their brother, Lazarus, wait excitedly at the door of their home for Jesus and his disciples to arrive. Martha has worked in the kitchen all day to make a feast good enough for a king. Mary is also planning to do something special for Jesus. She squeezes her hands together, feeling both happy and nervous.

THINK ABOUT IT!

Mary took a twelve-ounce jar of expensive perfume made from essence of nard, and she anointed Jesus' feet with it, wiping his feet with her hair. The house was filled with the fragrance.

John 12:3

Perfume was very expensive in Jesus' time. Often, it was made from ingredients only found in places that were far away from Israel. The perfume that Mary poured on Jesus' feet was made from an oil called *nard*. Nard comes from a flowering plant found high in the mountains of India and China. Nard was hard to get, so it was very valuable. It was often used to anoint royalty. When Mary anointed Jesus' feet with the perfume, she was not only showing her love and respect for Jesus, but she was also recognizing him as King.

Finally, there is a knock at the door, and Jesus and the disciples come in. The house is filled with happy hellos. "I hope you're hungry," Lazarus says to Jesus, giving him a big hug. Martha finishes welcoming the guests and hurries to bring in the food.

Everyone enjoys eating the delicious meal and being together as friends. Martha

watches proudly as the food she worked so hard on disappears from platters and plates. When Jesus has finished eating, Mary knows that it's her turn. She quietly gets up and leaves the room.

Mary soon returns, carrying a beautifully decorated jar. She walks over to the end of the couch that Jesus is lying on. Kneeling at his feet, she opens the jar. It is full of expensive perfume. Mary pours the perfume out onto Jesus' feet, filling the whole house with a beautiful fragrance. The other people in the room smell the perfume and turn to see what is happening. But Mary looks only at Jesus. She reaches up and takes off the veil covering her head, letting her hair fall down around her shoulders. Martha gasps, wondering why her sister is

showing her hair in a room full of men. Mary wipes the perfume from Jesus' feet with her long hair.

Judas Iscariot, one of Jesus' disciples, frowns. "What a waste!" he mutters to the people sitting near him. "That is the finest perfume. Someone would have to work an entire year to buy it! Mary should have sold the perfume and given the money to the poor."

But Jesus is smiling at Mary. "Leave her alone," he says. "Mary is getting me ready for my burial. There will always be poor people for you to help, but I will not be with you much longer."

To learn more about Mary anointing Jesus, read John 12:1-8.

Lana sighs and rests her head against the back of her seat. "I want to love Jesus like Mary did, not holding anything back," she says. The boys nod in agreement.

The bus's motor turns back on with a cough and sputter, ending the quiet moment. The bus makes a three-point turn in the narrow street and rumbles back the way it came.

"Back to Jerusalem again?" Munch asks.

"I think so," Griffin replies. The bus drives through the streets of Jerusalem and stops near the Temple.

Some important priests and captains of the Temple guard are huddled together, whispering.

"We have to get rid of this Jesus fellow," one of the priests says. "He's caused us enough trouble! It has to stop!"

"Just tell us when, and we'll arrest him," one of the guards says.

Another priest snorts. "We tried that already," he says, glaring at the guards. "You couldn't do it."

The guards look at each other. "He's too popular with the people," one of them mumbles. "We need to catch him when nobody's around."

"I can help you with that," a voice says. The priests and guards look around to see who is speaking. Judas Iscariot is leaning against the wall a little ways from the group. "I'm with Jesus all the time," he says. "I can tell you when he won't be surrounded by people."

The men look at Judas suspiciously. "You want to betray your teacher to us?" one of the priests asks. "What's in it for you?"

"How much will you pay me?" Judas asks. The men huddle up again and whisper together.

"Thirty pieces of silver," they offer.

"It's a deal," Judas says. "I'll tell you when to come arrest him." He looks around to make sure no one has seen him talking to the men, then walks away.

To learn more about Judas's betrayal, read Matthew 26:14-16; Mark 14:10-11; Luke 22:3-6.

All Together One Last Time

"Spinning sprockets!" Munch grips the back of the seat in front of him so hard that his hands shake. "I can't believe Judas would do that to Jesus!"

Griffin starts pacing the aisle of the bus. "I wish there was a way we could warn Jesus and the other disciples!"

"We can't." Lana's face is pale. "We can only watch."

The three friends are silent as the bus winds through the streets of Jerusalem and comes to a stop in front of a two-story house.

Baskets of flatbread sit on the table alongside bitter herbs and roasted lamb. Jesus and his disciples are getting ready to celebrate the Passover with the traditional meal. Jesus knows this is the last supper they will all share together before he must die for his people's sins.

The disciples enter the room and settle onto the couches lined up around the table. They talk to each other happily as they wait for the meal to begin.

Before everyone starts eating, Jesus gets up from the table, takes off his outer robe, and wraps a towel around his waist. The disciples watch, wondering what he is doing. Jesus pours water into a bowl and begins to wash his friends' feet.

THINK ABOUT IT!

The Last Supper was probably served on a U-shaped table called a *triclinium*. The people eating would be around the outer edge of the U, while the inside was left empty for servers to move around in. Instead of sitting on chairs, Jesus and his disciples most likely were stretched out on couches, with their heads toward the table and their feet away from it. They leaned on their left arms and used their right hands to pick up their food. John was likely sitting on Jesus' right, making it easy for him to lean back toward Jesus and speak to him privately. It's thought that Judas might have been sitting to Jesus' left, which would have allowed Jesus to hand him the piece of bread.

The men look at each other in shock. Washing feet is a job for a servant, not their teacher and Lord!

"No way!" Peter says when Jesus gets to him. "You are not going to wash my feet, Lord!"

Jesus smiles at Peter and tells him, "Unless I wash you, you won't belong to me."

"In that case, you'd better wash my hands and my head, too!" Peter exclaims.

"A person who has already bathed only needs to have his feet washed," Jesus says. "You disciples are clean—but not all of you." He puts on his robe and sits down again. "You call me your teacher and your Lord, because that's what I am. And since I have served you by washing your feet, you should serve each other in the same way."

Jesus and his disciples begin eating. Jesus looks around the table at his closest friends. "I've been looking forward to sharing this meal with you," he tells them. "But there is someone at this table who is going to betray me."

I am the vine; you are the branches. Those who remain in me, and I in them, will produce much fruit. For apart from me you can do nothing.
John 15:5

PARK HERE!
READ AND MEMORIZE THIS VERSE.

The disciples can't believe it. They look at each other and at Jesus, wondering which one of them Jesus could be talking about. Peter looks over at John and mouths, "Ask him who it is."

John leans over, close to Jesus. "Lord, who is it?" he whispers.

Jesus picks up a piece of bread. "It's the one that I will give this bread to after I dip it in the bowl." He dips the bread in a bowl of fruit paste and hands it to Judas Iscariot.

Judas takes the bread. "Am I the one, teacher?" he asks quietly.

"You have said it," Jesus says sadly. "Now go do what you're going to do."

Judas gets up from the table and disappears into the night.

Jesus gets everyone's attention. He picks up a piece of bread, thanks God for it, and breaks it into pieces, sharing it with the disciples. He says, "Take this and eat it. This is my body, which is given for you."

After supper is over, Jesus lifts up a cup of wine, thanks God for it, and says, “This is my blood, which will be poured out for many people so their sins may be forgiven.” Jesus drinks from the cup and then passes it around for all to share. Everyone takes a sip of the wine.

“My dear friends,” Jesus says, “it is time for me to finish my work and bring glory to God, my Father. I will only be with you a little while longer, and you can’t follow where I’m going to go.”

“Why not?” Peter asks, crossing his arms. “I’ll follow you anywhere. I’ll even die for you if I have to.”

Jesus shakes his head sadly. “Peter, before the rooster crows tomorrow morning, three times you will tell someone that you don’t even know me.”

“Impossible!” Peter insists. “I would never do that.”

The other disciples agree. “Me neither,” they all say.

Jesus gets up from the table. “It’s time to go,” he says. He leads his friends out of the room.

To learn more about the Last Supper, read Matthew 26:17-35; Mark 14:12-31; Luke 22:7-38; John 13–17.

Another Garden, Another Crossroads

The bus follows Jesus and his disciples up the Mount of Olives to the garden of Gethsemane. For once, its engine doesn't sputter, cough, or even rumble. The wheels don't make any noise on the rocky road.

When the bus stops, Lana gets out of her seat and goes to sit next to Griffin. Munch squeezes in next to her.

The moon shines down with silver light on Jesus and his 11 remaining friends. The olive trees in the garden make black, twisted shadows on the ground. "Peter, James, John," Jesus calls, "come with me. The rest of you stay here while I go and pray." The disciples have come to this spot with Jesus many times before. They find their favorite seats and get comfortable.

Peter, James, and John follow Jesus deeper into the garden. As they walk, Jesus becomes more and more upset. "My soul feels like it is being crushed with sadness," Jesus tells them. "Stay here and keep watch with me." Peter sits down under a tree and leans back against it. James and John stretch out on the grass. Jesus walks a little farther and then kneels down.

"Father," Jesus prays, "I know you can do anything. If there is any other way to carry out your plan, please don't let me go through the suffering that is ahead of me. But I will do whatever you want."

Jesus goes back to his friends. All three of them are fast asleep. Jesus bends down and shakes Peter. "Oh, Peter," Jesus says, "couldn't you keep me company even one hour?" Peter, James, and John are embarrassed. They straighten up and shake their heads, trying to stay awake.

Jesus goes off to pray by himself a second time. The next time he comes back to check on his disciples, they are asleep again. Jesus sighs and goes back to pray a third time. He is so upset and praying so hard that huge drops of sweat fall from his head to the ground. God sends an angel to help him stay strong.

When Jesus returns to his three friends, Peter, James, and John are all snoring again. They are so tired after the long and confusing day they have had. Jesus sits down next to them. "All right, then," he says. "Go ahead and rest." But then Jesus sees some flickering lights in the distance. He knows that they are torches held by the men who are coming to arrest him. He shakes his disciples awake. "Get up!" he tells them. "My betrayer is here."

Peter, James, and John jump to their feet. The other eight disciples come running. A large group of men with swords and torches is right behind them. The person in the lead is Judas.

Judas walks right up to Jesus. "Hello, teacher!" he says, kissing him. Before they arrived in the garden, Judas told the guards, "The man I kiss hello is the one you should arrest."

Jesus looks sadly at the friend who has decided to be his enemy. "Judas, are you really betraying me with a kiss?" he asks. Judas looks away.

Some of the men with Judas grab Jesus and start to tie his hands behind his back. "Get your hands off him!" Peter roars. He pulls out the sword he's been carrying and slashes at one of the men holding Jesus.

The man cries out and grabs the side of his head. "My ear!" he screams. "You cut off my ear!"

"Stop that, Peter," Jesus says. "Put your sword away." He reaches out and touches the man's ear—and heals it! Jesus looks around at all the men who have come to arrest him. "Am I a dangerous criminal?" he asks them. "Do you really need all these weapons?"

"Take him away!" shouts one of the guard captains. The men start to drag Jesus off. Jesus' disciples are afraid that they will be arrested too. They all run away, scattering into the darkness.

Following behind the soldiers, Judas watches as they mistreat his teacher. He feels the heavy pouch of money that the priests gave him and wonders if he made a mistake.

To learn more about Jesus being arrested, read Matthew 26:36-56; Mark 14:32-52; Luke 22:39-53; John 18:1-12.

Peter Trips Up

Lana, Griffin, and Munch watch with heavy hearts as Jesus is taken away. A few seconds later, Peter pops his head up from behind some bushes. "There's Peter!" Munch says. The bushes shake as Peter begins to move down the hill. "What's he doing?" Munch asks.

"He's following Jesus to see what happens to his teacher," Lana explains. "And look! John is with him."

Peter and John follow the soldiers to the house of Annas, the father-in-law of Caiaphas, the high priest. "I know Annas," John tells Peter. "Let me see if I can get us inside." Annas's house is surrounded by a wall. John walks up to the gate. The woman guarding the gate recognizes him and lets him in. "Please, may my friend come in too?" John asks. The woman agrees, and John beckons Peter over.

The woman stares at Peter as he walks through the gate. "Hey, are you one of Jesus' disciples?" she asks him.

"No," Peter says quickly, hurrying into the courtyard. A group of Annas's servants and guards have made a fire. Peter walks over and joins them. He's been out in the cold for a long time, and the heat feels nice.

Inside the house, Annas asks Jesus question after question, trying to get him to admit that he has done something wrong. Annas gets frustrated when he can't prove that Jesus has committed a crime. "Tie him up and take him to Caiaphas," Annas tells his guards. "He must be put on trial in front of the council."

Meanwhile, a servant girl has been staring at Peter by the light of

BUILD YOUR FAITH!

Despite being good friends with Jesus, Peter denied knowing him three times. Why do you think he did this? Have you ever said you weren't friends with someone because you were worried about what others might think? Has anyone ever done this to you? How did it make you feel?

the fire. "This man was with Jesus!" she tells the people next to her. "He's one of his closest friends!"

Peter's face turns red. "Woman, I don't even know Jesus," he says. He turns away, trying to hide his face.

A while later, a man comes up to Peter. "You must be one of Jesus' disciples," the man says. "I heard your accent—you talk like someone from Galilee, like Jesus."

"I don't know what you're talking about!" Peter cries. Before he's even finished speaking, he hears a rooster crow. Suddenly, movement in one of the windows of the house catches Peter's attention. Jesus is standing at the window, looking straight at Peter! Peter remembers what Jesus said—*"Peter, before the rooster crows tomorrow morning, three times you will tell someone that you don't even know me."*

Peter can't look at his Lord's face. He runs out of the courtyard, sobbing.

Jesus is taken to Caiaphas and the council. They try to find someone who can prove that Jesus has done something wrong, but they can't. They ask Jesus, "Are you the Messiah, God's chosen king?"

"You have said it," Jesus says. "And you will see me sitting in the place of power at God's right hand and coming on the clouds of heaven."

"We've heard enough!" the priests cry. "He is guilty!"

The council wants to kill Jesus, but only the Romans can kill criminals. So the council sends Jesus to the Roman governor, Pontius Pilate. Pilate talks to Jesus in his palace, then speaks to the council. By now a large crowd of people is standing outside, waiting to hear what Pilate will say.

"This man has not broken the law," Pilate says. "I think we should let him go."

"No way!" the priests shout. "He says he is a king! Only Caesar, the Roman emperor, is king! Kill Jesus! Kill him!"

"Well," Pilate says, "how about this: I always let one prisoner go free during the Passover. This year, I will release Jesus."

"No!" the priests yell. "Kill him! Release Barabbas instead!" The priests get all the people in the crowd to shout the same thing.

"But Barabbas is a dangerous man," Pilate says. "He's killed people!"

"Let Barabbas go! Kill Jesus!" the people shout.

Pilate is afraid that the crowd will start a riot. The emperor would be very angry if Pilate allowed fighting in the streets. Pilate could lose his job or even his life. "Bring me a bowl of water," he says to one of his servants. When the water arrives, Pilate washes his hands in front of all the people. "I'm doing this to show that Jesus' death is not my fault," he tells them. "It's your choice. His blood will not be on my hands."

"Fine!" the people yell.

"Okay then," Pilate says. He orders that Jesus be flogged with a lead-tipped whip and then crucified, or killed by being nailed on a cross.

To learn more about Jesus' trial and Peter's denial, read Matthew 26:57–27:26; Mark 14:53–15:15; Luke 22:54–23:25; John 18:13–19:16.

The Place of the Skull

Sharp thorns dig into Jesus' head, and blood trickles down his forehead. Pilate's soldiers stand in a circle around him. They tease Jesus and make fun of him. Placing a purple robe around his shoulders, they say, "Here you go, Your Highness." They hit Jesus and spit in his face.

When the soldiers get tired of mocking Jesus, they take off the purple robe and put his own clothes back on him. Jesus is exhausted from being up all night and already badly hurt from the terrible whipping the soldiers gave him. But his awful journey is just beginning.

"Hey, you!" the soldiers shout at a man who is passing by. "Come over here and carry this cross! We need to get it all the way up to the Place of the Skull, and the King of the

Jews here can't carry it himself. The man's name is Simon, and he is visiting Jerusalem from his home in northern Africa. He comes over and picks up the heavy wooden beam that will be attached to a tall post to make the cross.

Up on the hill called the Place of the Skull, the soldiers nail Jesus' hands to the wood beam. Once they lift him up onto the post, it gets harder and harder for him to breathe. The soldiers nail his feet to the post.

Jesus is dying and in horrible pain, but his love is still the strongest thing there is. The priests and the people in the crowd make fun of him as they watch him die. The Roman soldiers who are hurting him laugh at him and steal his clothing. But instead of getting angry, Jesus prays for them. "Father, forgive them," he calls out to God. "They do not understand what they are doing."

Two criminals are being crucified with Jesus—one on each side. One of them makes fun of Jesus along with everyone else. But the other one recognizes that Jesus is a great King. "I deserve to die for the bad things I've done, but you've never done anything wrong," the man says to Jesus. "Please remember me when you get to your Kingdom."

Jesus looks over at the dying man with love. "I promise that you will come to heaven with me today," he tells him.

A group of women who love Jesus, including his mother, his aunt, and his friend Mary Magdalene, stand near the cross, tears running down their faces. John is there as well. Jesus looks at his mother. "Dear woman," he says, "John will be your son now." He turns to John. "Take care of my mother," he says.

The sky turns black, even though it is the middle of the afternoon. The ground trembles and shakes. "It is finished!" Jesus shouts. "Father, I give you my spirit." He takes his final breath and dies.

Nicodemus, the man who visited Jesus in the middle of the night,

and his friend Joseph go to Pilate and ask if they can bury Jesus. Joseph has a tomb that they can use. Pilate orders some soldiers to take Jesus' body down from the cross and give it to Nicodemus and Joseph. The two men wrap the body carefully with cloth and spices and place it in the tomb. Then they roll a giant rock in front of the entrance to the tomb.

Mary Magdalene and another woman named Mary follow Nicodemus and Joseph to find out where Jesus is being buried. They want to make sure that Jesus' body is being cared for properly. But it is getting late, and the women need to go home. "We will come back after the day of rest is over," they say.

The next day, the priests go to see Pilate. "That liar Jesus used to say that he would rise from the dead," they tell the governor. "You had better put some guards on his tomb so that his followers don't steal his body and try to trick people into thinking that he came back to life."

Pilate sends some soldiers to guard the tomb. "No one is getting in—or out!" they say.

To learn more about Jesus' crucifixion and burial, read Matthew 27:27-66; Mark 15:16-47; Luke 23:26-56; John 19:17-42.

Griffin, Lana, and Munch don't seem to realize that they're holding hands, squeezing as tightly as they can. They don't speak or look at each other as fog hides the view out the bus windows.

Finally Munch clears his throat. "Are we time traveling again?" he asks. Griffin shrugs.

The fog clears, revealing a dark-gray world. The sky in the east is just starting to get lighter. Lana launches herself at the window, almost landing on Griffin.

"Oh, I hope it's Sunday!" she says.

It's early Sunday morning, and everything is quiet at the tomb. The guards are alert, watching for thieves. Suddenly, the ground starts shaking. An angel, with a face as bright as lightning and clothes as

BUILD YOUR FAITH!

The word *gospel* means "good news." The gospel of Jesus is the Good News that he died for us on the cross so that our sins may be forgiven. Jesus' resurrection demonstrates that God is stronger than sin and death! God promises that everyone who believes in him will live with him forever. Have you asked God to forgive you for your sins? He wants to be your forever friend.

white as snow, comes down from heaven. He grabs the stone in front of the tomb and rolls it aside as if it doesn't weigh a thing. Then he sits down on top of the stone. The guards tremble and then faint in terror!

Meanwhile, Mary Magdalene, the other Mary, and some of their friends are on their way to the tomb. They want to put more spices on Jesus' body and make sure he has been properly prepared for burial. "How will we roll aside that huge stone?" one Mary asks.

"Maybe we should have brought some more people with us," the other Mary says.

But the stone has already been rolled away, and there's an angel at the tomb! The women cry out in fear and shock.

"Don't be afraid," the angel says. "This is a place for dead people, so why are you looking here for someone who is alive? Jesus isn't here! He has risen! Go and tell his friends!"

He is risen from the dead, just as he said would happen.

Matthew 28:6

PARK HERE!

READ AND MEMORIZE THIS VERSE.

The women can't believe it! They look at each other, laughing and crying with joy and fear at the same time. Then they rush off to tell everyone they can find.

Mary Magdalene runs to find Peter and John. "The tomb is empty! Jesus isn't there!" she yells. Peter and John run to the tomb as fast as they can. John is faster and gets to the tomb first. He peers in through the doorway and sees the cloths that were wrapped around Jesus' body. Then Peter dashes up, huffing and puffing, and pushes past John, going right into the tomb. He looks at the empty cloths too.

John finally comes all the way into the tomb. "Jesus is alive," he whispers. The two men aren't sure what to do next, so they go home.

But Mary Magdalene stays, standing outside the tomb. She is feeling so many different things that she doesn't know what to think. *If Jesus is really alive, where is he?* she wonders. *What if someone stole his body after all?* Mary starts to cry again.

Through her tears, Mary sees a man walking toward her. She thinks he must be a gardener who takes care of the land around the tomb. "Dear woman, why are you crying?" the man asks. His voice is kind.

"If you took him away, just tell me where he is," Mary sobs. "I will go get him."

"Mary!" the man says. Suddenly Mary knows who he is.

"Teacher!" she gasps. Now she is crying happy tears instead of sad ones.

"Go and tell my friends that you have seen me," Jesus tells her. Mary happily obeys.

That night the disciples are meeting together in a locked room. They are afraid that the Romans will come and arrest them, too. Suddenly Jesus is standing right there with them! "Peace be with you," he says. He lets his friends touch the wounds that the nails made in his hands, so that they will know it is really him. He eats some food to show that he is not a ghost. The disciples are filled with joy. Their Lord is alive!

To learn more about Jesus' resurrection, read Matthew 28:1-10; Mark 16:1-14; Luke 24:1-43; John 20–21.

"YES!" Munch shouts, pumping his fist in the air. Lana and Griffin give each other high fives. Then they have to grab onto their seats as the bus lurches into motion again.

Griffin snatches up the map. "Back to the Mount of Olives," he tells his friends.

It has been 40 days since Jesus rose from the dead, and he has spent a lot of time with his followers, showing them that he is alive and teaching them about how they should live for him. One day, he brings them to the Mount of Olives. "It is time for me to go back to my

Father," he tells them. "You will continue my work. I will send my Holy Spirit to you, and he will give you the power to tell people about me, both here in Jerusalem and all over the world."

Suddenly Jesus is taken up to heaven in a cloud. The disciples keep staring into the sky for a long time after he disappears. All of a sudden they notice that two men dressed in white are standing with them. "Why are you standing here looking at the sky?" the men ask. "Jesus has gone into heaven, but someday he will come back!"

To learn more about Jesus' ascension to heaven, read Mark 16:15-20; Luke 24:50-53; Acts 1:4-12.

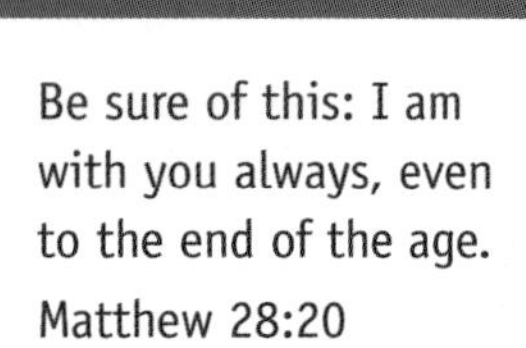

Be sure of this: I am with you always, even to the end of the age.
Matthew 28:20

PARK HERE!
READ AND MEMORIZE THIS VERSE.

"Spinning sprockets!" Munch shouts.

Lana doesn't say anything, but there is a huge smile across her face. The bus chugs down the hill, back into the city of Jerusalem. It pulls over next to a house.

"Look!" Munch says, pointing to the second-story window. "There's a bunch of people sitting together in the upstairs room."

"It's Pentecost," Lana explains, looking in the Bible. "All of Jesus' followers have gathered to celebrate the Jewish festival."

Mary, Jesus' mother, looks around the room happily. She loves being with all the people who love her son. Suddenly a deafening noise makes her jump. "What is that?" Mary asks, covering her ears.

"It sounds like a windstorm," Peter says, looking out the window.

The friends glance at each other nervously. "Should we take cover?" someone asks. But before Peter can answer, the wind bursts through the window and whips across the room.

Mary stares at a flame of fire that has settled above Peter's head. Looking around, she sees that there are flames above each of the believers' heads. Everyone in the room realizes that they have been filled with the Holy Spirit. The friends begin to praise God, but they do not recognize the words that come from their mouths. God's Spirit is giving them the ability to speak in languages that they don't know.

BUILD YOUR FAITH!

If you have trusted Jesus as your Savior, you are filled with the Holy Spirit! The Holy Spirit can lead and guide you to do what is pleasing to God. The Holy Spirit even prays for you when you don't know what to pray (see Romans 8:26). The next time you feel alone or confused, remember that God's own Spirit is with you, ready to help!

Hearing the loud wind, the people of Jerusalem come running to the house to see what is happening. They are shocked when they hear Jesus' followers speaking in foreign languages. People have come to Jerusalem from many different countries to celebrate Pentecost, and everyone hears someone speaking in his or her native language! "Jesus' friends are ordinary people from Galilee," one of them says. "How is it possible that they are speaking in all of these different languages?"

But other people do not want to believe that God is doing a miracle. "They're just babbling nonsense!" someone shouts. "They've been drinking too much wine!"

Peter steps forward and says to the crowd, "Listen, everyone! These people aren't full of alcohol. They are full of God's Holy Spirit!" The crowd grows quiet. Everyone listens carefully to every word Peter says. "You all know that God did many powerful miracles through Jesus. But you killed Jesus by nailing him to the cross. But God didn't leave him in the tomb—he raised him from the dead! You can be sure of this—God has made Jesus, the one you crucified, the Lord and Messiah."

Peter's words touch the hearts of the people. They ask the apostles, "What should we do?"

"Ask God to forgive your sins," Peter says. "Be baptized in the name of Jesus. Then you also will be given the Holy Spirit."

Peter preaches to the crowd for a long time. By the time he finishes, 3,000 more people believe in Jesus!

To learn more about the arrival of the Holy Spirit at Pentecost, read Acts 2:1-41.

No Turning Back

As the number of believers grows, so do the chores of the 12 apostles. The believers want to make sure that they are taking care of the widows and other people who don't have enough food to eat. They all share what they have so that everyone will have what they need. But making sure that everything is passed out fairly is a very big job. Some people start to complain that they aren't getting enough food, and the apostles find that they don't have time for anything else.

The 12 apostles call all the believers to meet together. "Passing out food is an important job, but we apostles need to focus on teaching God's Word," they say. "Let's choose seven men who are wise and filled with God's Spirit. They will be in charge of making sure that everyone is taken care of." Everyone agrees that this is a good idea.

One of the men chosen to help is named Stephen, and he is full of faith and the Holy Spirit. God gives him the ability to do many amazing miracles. When some Jews come to argue with him, Stephen's answers are so wise that he wins every argument. This makes the Jews very angry. So they lie to get Stephen in trouble.

"This man is saying bad things about God!" they tell the religious leaders. "Do something about it!" The religious leaders arrest Stephen and bring him in front of the high council.

"What do you have to say for yourself?" the high priest asks Stephen. Stephen answers by telling how God has always been faithful to his people, even though they disobey him again and again. Finally

Stephen says, "You are such stubborn people, just like your ancestors! Why do you fight against the Holy Spirit? Your ancestors killed God's messengers, the prophets—and you killed Jesus, God's Messiah, the Savior."

Stephen's words make the religious leaders furious. They shake their fists at Stephen in rage. But Stephen stays focused on God. Looking toward heaven, he sees Jesus. "Look!" Stephen says, pointing up. "I see Jesus, and he is standing at God's right hand, being honored."

This makes the leaders angry enough to

THINK ABOUT IT!

All the believers met together in one place and shared everything they had.
Acts 2:44

The first believers in Jesus—the apostles and his other followers—are sometimes called "the early church." The members of the early church shared everything. They prayed together, ate together, and looked after each other's needs. Some members of the early church sold their land and belongings, giving the money to the apostles to distribute to the needy within the group. They did this to demonstrate their love for Jesus and each other.

SLOW!

kill. They rush at Stephen and drag him out of the city. They begin to throw stones at Stephen.

Stephen's attackers take off their coats so they can throw more easily. "I'll watch the coats," a young man named Saul says.

Stone after stone strikes Stephen. He prays, "Lord Jesus, receive my spirit." Then he forgives his killers, calling out, "Lord, do not charge them with this sin!" And then Stephen dies.

When Saul sees that Stephen is dead, he nods with approval. *Stephen got what he deserved*, Saul thinks. *We need to get rid of all of these followers of Jesus*.

Saul becomes the number-one enemy of the believers in Jesus. He goes all over Jerusalem, dragging every believer he can find to jail. Many of Jesus' followers run away from the city, terrified that Saul will catch them next.

To learn more about Stephen, read Acts 6:1–8:3.

Something Strange Happens on the Way to Damascus

"Man, when is God going to do something about that Saul guy?" Munch clenches his fists as the bus starts up.

"Don't worry, Munch," Griffin says. "If I'm right, we're heading to Damascus, which means we're about to see Jesus do something about Saul." After a while, a group of men comes into view. "Yep, this is it," Griffin says. "Watch."

Munch crosses his arms and leans back in his seat. "I can't wait."

Even though he's been traveling for several days, Saul is still in a hurry. His sandals kick up dust as he rushes toward the city of Damascus. The men traveling with him are sweating and breathing hard, struggling to keep up. "Come on!" Saul calls over his shoulder. "We can't waste any time. We need to stop these dangerous Jesus followers who are messing up our religion. I'm going to arrest every single man and woman who follows Jesus and bring them back to Jerusalem in chains." Saul scowls as he thinks about how much he hates the believers.

Saul squints at the outline of Damascus up ahead. "We're almost there!" he says, walking even faster. But before Saul can take more than a few steps, a blinding white light shoots out of the sky and surrounds him. Saul tumbles to the ground, trying to protect his eyes.

A voice echoes out of nowhere. "Saul! Saul! Why are you hurting me?"

"Who's talking?" Saul asks. His eyes are clenched shut.

"It's me, Jesus—the one you are hurting," the voice says. "Now get up. Go to Damascus and wait for me to tell you what to do next."

Saul's friends look at each other, too shocked to speak. They heard a voice, but they didn't see anyone talking. Saul picks himself up off the ground, but when he opens

DAMASCUS

- Damascus is the capital of the modern country of Syria. It is one of the oldest cities in the world.
- When the Romans conquered Damascus in the first century BC, they completely redesigned the city. Paul would have seen the Roman buildings, some of which are still standing today.
- The area around Damascus is mostly desert. Summers are hot, and winters are mild.
- Foods produced in Damascus include figs, dates, olives, watermelons, garlic, onions, and lamb.

Fun Fact: During the Middle Ages, Damascus was well known for making swords and lace.

his eyes, he can't see a thing. "Help!" he cries. "I'm blind!" Saul's friends scurry over to him. They take him by the hands and lead him to Damascus. For three days, Saul is blind and does not eat or drink anything.

But God has a plan for Saul. A follower of Jesus named Ananias lives in Damascus. God speaks to Ananias in a vision. "Ananias!" God calls.

"Yes, Lord!" Ananias replies.

"Go to the house of Judas," God tells him. "Ask for a man named Saul. He is there praying. I have shown him in a vision that a man named Ananias will come and help him see again."

"What?" Ananias exclaims. "I've heard of Saul! He's evil! He wants to arrest all of your followers."

"I have chosen Saul to be my messenger," God says.

THINK ABOUT IT!

Joseph [was] the one the apostles nicknamed Barnabas (which means "Son of Encouragement").

Acts 4:36

Barnabas was one of the early leaders of the church. His real name was Joseph; *Barnabas* was probably a nickname. Barnabas noticed the good things people were doing for Jesus and told everyone about them. He gave people a chance when other people didn't trust them. When Paul became a Christian, Barnabas introduced him to the apostles. Later, Paul and Barnabas lived together in Antioch teaching many Gentiles (non-Jewish people) how to become believers. Together, they traveled to many cities, helping the early church to grow.

Ananias obeys God and goes to see Saul. When he arrives, he places his hands on Saul and says, "Brother Saul, Jesus has sent me so that you may see again and be filled with the Holy Spirit." Instantly, something like fish scales falls from Saul's eyes and he can see. Saul is immediately baptized to show that he is a follower of Jesus.

Saul is so excited about his new faith that he begins to preach about Jesus in the synagogues, where Jews meet to worship God. "Who does this Saul guy think he is?" the Jews ask. "Look at him! First, he was going to arrest anyone who followed Jesus. Now, he is one of Jesus' followers." Saul's teaching is so powerful that it makes some of the Jews very angry, and they start to plan how they can kill him.

Someone tells Saul that he is in danger, and the believers help him escape from Damascus. Saul climbs into a large basket, and his friends lower it from an opening in the city wall. Saul goes to Jerusalem and tries to meet with Jesus' followers there. But the believers in Jerusalem do not believe that Saul is really on Jesus' side now. They are afraid that Saul is trying to trick them.

Finally, a man named Barnabas takes a chance. He brings Saul to the apostles and tells them about how Saul met Jesus on the way to Damascus. The apostles decide that Saul is really a believer. Their biggest enemy has become their friend!

To learn more about Saul becoming a follower of Jesus, read Acts 9:1-31.

Another Journey Back from the Grave

"Well, that wasn't exactly what I was expecting," Munch says as the bus leaves Jerusalem, "but it was pretty cool." Griffin and Lana smile at each other.

After a while, the bus drives into a coastal town. "This place looks familiar," Lana says.

"That's because we've been here before," Griffin says. "When we saw Jonah. We're back in Joppa."

Peter walks down a crooked path that leads to a small house in the town of Joppa. The two men with him run ahead, into the house and up the stairs. A group of people crowds into a small room on the upper floor. They all look very sad. Some of them cry quietly, tears running down their cheeks. Others sob loudly.

“We found Peter!” the two men tell their friends. “He is right behind us!” Peter enters the room, and the people surround him.

“Isn’t this coat lovely?” one woman asks. “Tabitha made it for me when I had no coat to wear.”

“She made my clothes too,” another woman says. “When my husband died, I thought I would be all alone. But Tabitha has been my friend. She made sure I had everything I needed.”

The women start to cry even more loudly. "What will we do without Tabitha?" they sob.

Peter looks around at all the sad faces. He can tell that Tabitha both gave and received a lot of love while she was alive. "Please, everybody leave the room," he says gently.

Tabitha's friends don't know why Peter is asking them to leave, but they obey and go downstairs. Alone in the room, Peter kneels down next to Tabitha's body, which is lying on her bed. He prays to God.

When he is finished praying, Peter turns to the body. "Get up, Tabitha," he says softly. And Tabitha opens her eyes! She looks at Peter and sits up in surprise.

"Peter!" she says. "What are you doing here?"

Peter smiles. "Welcome back, Tabitha," he says. He gives her his hand and helps her stand up. "Your friends will be very happy to see you."

Peter calls Tabitha's friends back into the room. When they come in, they can't believe their eyes! The women run to Tabitha and hug her, crying happy tears. "You're alive! You're alive!" they say.

Soon everyone in Joppa has heard the news. Many people believe in Jesus. "If he has the power to bring back the dead, he must really be God's Son!" they say.

To learn more about Peter raising Tabitha, read Acts 9:36-42.

An Unexpected Traveling Companion

"Spinning sprockets!" Munch exclaims. "Jesus gave Peter the power to bring that woman back from the dead!"

The bus rumbles out of Joppa, traveling up the coast. Eventually it reaches a large city with many beautiful buildings. "Wow!" Lana says, admiring the architecture. "We haven't been here before."

"This is Caesarea," Griffin tells his friends.

In a house in Caesarea, a man dressed in a Roman army uniform is kneeling on the floor, his head bowed in prayer. His name is Cornelius, and he prays like this every day. But today something very unusual happens. When Cornelius opens his eyes and looks up, he sees an angel walking toward him! "Cornelius!" the angel says.

Cornelius stares at the angel. As a Roman officer, he has faced many dangers bravely, but the sight of this messenger from heaven makes him tremble with fear. "What can I do for you, sir?" he asks.

"God has noticed your prayers and the way you help the poor," the angel replies. "Now send some of your men to Joppa to find a man named Peter." Then the angel disappears.

Cornelius doesn't waste a single minute. He calls for two of his servants and one of his most trusted soldiers. "Go to Joppa and bring back a man named Peter," he tells them. "He has an important message for me."

The three men set out to find Peter. Cornelius waits for several days. On the day that the travelers are expected to return, Cornelius calls together all of his family and friends. "You must hear what this man Peter has to say!" he tells them. Cornelius paces back and forth and peers out the window down the road. Finally he sees a group of people

CAESAREA

- Caesarea is located along the coast of the Mediterranean Sea. It is still a city in the modern country of Israel.
- Caesarea was built by King Herod the Great in 25–13 BC as a gift to the Roman emperor Caesar Augustus. It had one of the largest harbors in the ancient world.
- The land around Caesarea and its warm and rainy climate were very good for producing crops. Many orchards were planted around the city.

Fun Fact: Caesarea is the city where Pontius Pilate ruled and lived during the time of Jesus.

coming up to the house. Cornelius recognizes the three men he sent, traveling with several strangers. One of them must be Peter! Cornelius races out to meet them.

"Master! Here is Peter!" one of Cornelius's servants says, pointing to one of the strangers. Cornelius falls to the dusty ground, bowing down in front of Peter.

But Peter grabs his shoulders and lifts him up. "Stand up!" he says. "I'm a human being just like you." Cornelius brings the travelers inside, where his friends and relatives are waiting.

Peter looks around at the people who have gathered to listen to him. "This is the first time I have been in the home of a Gentile, a non-Jewish person," Peter says. "You know that it is against the law for a Jewish man to be friends with Gentiles or visit their homes. But God showed me a vision while I was in Joppa, telling me that I should

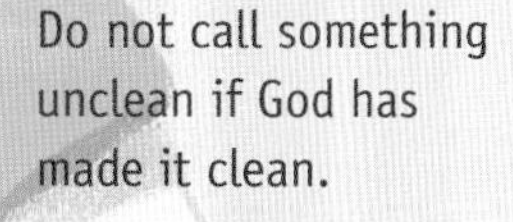

Do not call something unclean if God has made it clean.

Acts 10:15

not think of anyone as being impure or unclean. So here I am. Now tell me," Peter says, turning to Cornelius, "why did you ask me to come?"

Cornelius tells Peter about the angel who visited him and then says, "Thank you for coming. We are all waiting to hear what God wants to say to us through you."

"I understand now that God loves all people," Peter says. "Everyone who believes in Jesus will have his or her sins forgiven, including the Gentiles." Peter explains the Good News that Jesus died and came back to life to save people from their sins. As he is speaking, the Gentiles believe in Jesus and are filled with the Holy Spirit. The Jewish believers who are with Peter watch in amazement.

"Nobody can disagree that these Gentiles should be baptized and join the church," Peter says to the Jewish believers. "They are truly our brothers and sisters, because they have received the Holy Spirit just like we did." The new believers are baptized, and Cornelius invites Peter and his friends to stay for a while and talk more about Jesus.

To learn more about Cornelius, read Acts 10.

BUILD YOUR FAITH!

God showed Peter that everyone is welcome in God's Kingdom. While all of God's creations are very good, they are also very different from one another. God made people of all shapes, sizes, and colors. He gave them different gifts and talents. God loves everyone and welcomes them all to be his friends. Think of someone who is different from you. What are some things about that person that God made unique and special? How could you celebrate your differences?

Peter "Dreams" of Escape

"Jesus' message is for everyone, no matter where they come from!" Lana says excitedly as the bus pulls away from Cornelius's house. "Griffin, where are we going next?"

Griffin looks at the map. "Looks like it's back to—"

"Let me guess," Munch interrupts. "Jerusalem."

"Hey, you!" a voice shouts behind Peter. Before he can even turn around, several pairs of hands grab him roughly from behind. King Herod's soldiers yank Peter's hands behind his back and clamp chains around his wrists. "You're under arrest, by order of King Herod," one of the soldiers says.

The believers who are with Peter watch in horror. "Oh no," one of them whispers. "Not Peter, too! We just lost James!"

THINK ABOUT IT!

"I'd like to hear [Paul] myself," [Herod] Agrippa said.
Acts 25:22

There are five different Herods mentioned in the Bible. All of them were related to each other. Herod the Great was the king the wise men visited. Herod Philip II, one of Herod the Great's sons, ruled an area northeast of the Sea of Galilee after his father's death. Another of Herod the Great's sons, Herod Antipas, was the king mentioned during the time of Jesus' crucifixion. Herod Agrippa I was the nephew of Herod Antipas. He was the king who had the apostle James killed. The last Herod who appears in the Bible is Herod Agrippa II. He was the son of Herod Agrippa I, and he listened to Paul's testimony after Paul was arrested in Jerusalem.

SLOW!

King Herod recently had the apostle James killed to please the Jewish people that he rules. Many Jewish people hate those who believe in Jesus because they think the believers are ruining the Jewish religion and causing trouble with the Romans.

The soldiers drag Peter away. "We will pray for you, Peter!" his friends call. The soldiers bring Peter before King Herod. The king is pacing back and forth, watching anxiously for the soldiers. A big smile spreads across his face when he sees Peter in chains. "I made everyone so happy by killing James," he says. "Imagine how they will celebrate when I kill you!" Herod turns to the soldiers. "Throw him in prison, and put 16 soldiers in charge of guarding him," the king says. "Make sure there's no way he can escape! I'll hold a public trial for him after Passover."

The night before he is supposed to be put on trial, Peter tries to sleep in his prison cell. *These chains sure are uncomfortable,* Peter thinks, tugging at his wrists. He is chained between two guards. The other guards standing at the door shoot him nasty looks. Peter smiles back. After a lot of shifting around, Peter is finally able to fall asleep.

Thwack! What feels like just a short time

later, Peter is awakened by someone walloping him in the side. When he opens his eyes, he has to squint because his prison cell is filled with a blinding light. *Is it time for the trial already?* Peter wonders. But then he sees that an angel is standing next to him! *Oh, I must be dreaming,* Peter thinks. *God has sent me a vision of an angel.*

"Quick! Get up!" the angel tells Peter. Peter watches as the chains on his wrists open up and fall off, all by themselves. *Now I know I am dreaming,* he thinks.

"Get dressed and follow me," the angel says. Peter hurries to put on his coat and sandals. He follows as the angel leads him past the guard posts, outside the big iron gate, and into the streets of Jerusalem. And then the angel just disappears. Peter looks around the darkened street, expecting that any second he will wake up and find himself back in his prison cell. *That was a strange dream,* he thinks. He waits. Then he waits some more. Finally he realizes that the road beneath his feet is solid and the night breeze feels cool on his skin. "Wow!" Peter says. "I wasn't dreaming at all. I am actually free! God sent an angel to save me from Herod."

Peter takes off down the road. He wants to find his fellow believers and let them know that he is okay. He heads toward the home of Mary, the mother of John Mark. Jesus' followers often gather there to pray. Soon Peter arrives at the house and taps gently on the door. After a moment, he hears footsteps on the other side of the door. "Who is it?" calls a voice. It's Mary's servant Rhoda.

"Rhoda, it's me, Peter," Peter says. "Open the door." He hears a gasp, followed by footsteps running away. *Why isn't she opening the door?* Peter wonders. He keeps knocking.

After what feels like a very long time, someone finally opens the door. Peter comes in and is immediately surrounded by his friends. "We didn't believe it when Rhoda said it was you!" someone says.

"It is amazing," Peter agrees. "I thought it was a dream at first." Then he tells everyone about his miraculous escape.

To learn more about Peter's escape from prison, read Acts 12:1-19.

Griffin consults the map as the bus gets moving again. "Looks like we're going to a city called Antioch," he tells his friends.

"Antioch!" Lana exclaims. "Barnabas and Saul worked in a church there!" She flips through the Bible. "Or Paul, I guess we should call him. That's his Gentile name, and the one most people know him by."

"Yeah, I've heard of Paul," Munch says. "You mean the apostle Paul and that guy Saul are the same person?"

"Yep," Lana replies. "And there he is!"

Paul and Barnabas shove clothes and food into sacks, bags, and chests. They are packing up their belongings for a long trip. A few days earlier, they were praying and fasting with their friends Simeon, Lucius, and Manaen when something extraordinary happened. The Holy Spirit told the men that Paul and Barnabas had been chosen for a special mission. So now they are traveling to the island of Cyprus to help spread God's Word.

ANTIOCH

- Antioch is also called "Antioch on the Orontes" or "Syrian Antioch." The ruins of this ancient city are located near the modern city of Antakya, Turkey.
- Antioch was located along the Orontes River, on a major trading route between Rome and the countries to the east of the empire.
- The city of Antioch was founded by one of Alexander the Great's generals. It was an important city in the Roman Empire and an important city in the history of Christianity. Paul lived there for 14 years.
- The weather in Antioch was usually warm and mild. People in Antioch fished for food and also ate wheat, vegetables, and fruits.
- Antioch had many forests. The wood cut from them was used for building.

Fun Fact: The followers of Jesus were first called Christians in Antioch (see Acts 11:26).

"Here we go!" Lana shouts, bouncing in her seat. "Paul's first missionary journey!"

Munch looks over Griffin's shoulder at the map. "Where's Cyprus?" he asks.

"There it is." Griffin points.

"Um . . . that's an island," Munch says. "How is this bus going to cross the ocean?"

Just then, the bus reaches the seashore and starts splashing into the water. The three friends hold their breath. Suddenly, the wheels retract and a huge inflatable raft pops out of the bottom of the bus. The bus's engine revs, and it starts motoring across the waves.

"Spinning sprockets!" Munch yells. "How cool is this?"

"What's our plan?" Paul asks the minute he and Barnabas step off the boat.

"Let's start here in the town of Salamis and then preach to every Jewish synagogue on the island," Barnabas says. "We'll end near the town of Paphos."

"Great idea!" Paul says. The two men, along with their assistant, John Mark, set out to spread the word about God's Kingdom.

When they reach the town of Paphos, the governor, Sergius

CYPRUS

- Cyprus is a large island in the Mediterranean Sea, located near Turkey.
- Many nations thought that Cyprus was important and wanted to control it.
- Cyprus was known for producing wine, oil, and corn. It also had many minerals and natural resources, including copper and timber.
- Cyprus's climate is subtropical, with hot, dry summers and mild, wet winters.

Fun Fact: Cyprus was the home of Barnabas, who traveled with Paul on missionary trips.

Paulus, sends for them. “I have been wanting to hear God’s Word,” the governor says. Paul and Barnabas can tell that he is an intelligent man.

But Paul and Barnabas haven’t been speaking long when the doors of the room they are in open with a crash. “Don’t listen to these men, Governor!” someone yells. “They don’t know what they are talking about.” It is Elymas, a Jewish sorcerer who hangs around the governor.

Paul, filled with the Holy Spirit, looks Elymas right in the eye.

Paul's Letters

A lot of the New Testament is made up of letters written from church leaders to believers in different parts of the world. Most of the New Testament letters, or Epistles, were written by Paul. Paul's letters are named after the people he wrote them to—mostly churches but some individuals (Timothy, Titus, and Philemon). The other Epistles, except for Hebrews, are named for the person who wrote them (Jesus' brothers James and Jude; the apostles Peter and John). Hebrews is also named for its recipients, because we don't know for sure who wrote it.

Rome
Philippi
Thessalonica
Galatia
Ephesus
Corinth
Colossae
N
W
E
S

"You're lying!" Paul shouts. "The Lord will punish you by making you blind."

Immediately mist and darkness come over Elymas's eyes. "Help me!" the sorcerer begs. "I can't see."

Sergius Paulus is amazed at God's power. "Now I know that Paul and Barnabas are telling the truth," he says. The governor becomes a follower of Jesus.

To learn more about Paul's first missionary journey, read Acts 13:1-12.

God Opens the Doors for Paul and Silas

The bus speeds back over the waves to the mainland. Once back on dry land, it travels for a long time. "We're heading northwest," Griffin informs Lana and Munch.

Finally, a sign comes into view out the bus window. It reads, "Philippi."

"There's Paul!" Munch says, pointing out the window. "But who are those guys with him? And I don't see Barnabas."

Lana looks at the Bible. "This must be Paul's second missionary journey," she says. "I bet those men are Silas and Luke."

"Then who is the girl following them?" Munch asks.

"These men are servants of the Most High God!" the girl yells, waving her arms wildly in the air. She dances crazily in the street behind Paul, Silas, and Luke. "They have come to tell you how to be saved!" For days the girl has been following the three men around everywhere they go.

The girl is a slave, both to human masters and the evil spirit living inside her. The spirit tells her things that ordinary people couldn't know. Her human masters use this ability to make money. They claim that she is a fortune-teller and charge people a fee to hear what the girl has to say about them.

"I can't take this anymore!" Paul says to Silas and Luke. He turns toward the slave girl and says, "Demon, leave this girl at once in the name of Jesus Christ!" The demon instantly leaves the girl.

The girl is relieved, but her masters are not. They are angry because without the demon, the girl cannot tell fortunes, and they won't make any more money. They grab Paul and Silas, separating them from Luke, and drag them over to the city officials. "Throw these men in jail!" they shout. "They are causing trouble all over our city!" A mob forms, and the crowd shouts insults at Paul and Silas. The city officials order that the two men be beaten with wooden rods and thrown in prison.

"Make sure these men don't escape!" the officials tell the jailer.

PHILIPPI

- Philippi was a city in eastern Macedonia, founded by King Philip II. It was the site of the famous Roman battle in which Mark Antony and Octavian defeated Brutus and Cassius.
- Paul visited Philippi during his second and third missionary trips.
- In Paul's time, the city did not have a synagogue. Instead Jews worshiped near the Gangites River. Paul and Silas met a Jewish woman named Lydia near the river, and she became one of the first Philippians to become a Christian.
- Philippi was surrounded by mountains and fertile plains.

Fun Fact: In its early years, Philippi was a gold rush city. People came there to mine gold in the nearby mountains.

"You can count on me," the jailer promises. He locks Paul and Silas in the farthest, deepest dungeon and clamps their feet into stocks.

"Well," Paul says to Silas, "I guess God is making sure that we don't forget to take time to pray and sing to him."

Silas chuckles, then puts his hand to his bruised side. "Ouch! Don't make me laugh, Paul!"

Paul and Silas do pray and sing hymns to God. The other prisoners quiet down so they can listen. Around midnight, a tremor runs through the jail. "Did you feel that?" Silas asks Paul.

Both men fall over on their sides as the earth begins to shake. "Earthquake!" Paul shouts. All of a sudden, the doors of the prison cells fly open, and the chains fall off of all the prisoners.

Always be full of joy in the Lord. I say it again—rejoice!

Philippians 4:4

The shaking wakes the jailer, and he comes running. He cries out when he sees all the cell doors standing wide open. "Oh, no!" he says, drawing his sword. "The city officials will say it is my fault that all the prisoners escaped. I had better kill myself now, or they will do worse things to me."

Paul sees the jailer take out his sword. "Stop!" he shouts. "Don't hurt yourself. We did not escape. We are right here."

The jailer runs into the dungeon and falls on the ground in front of Paul and Silas, shaking. "What must I do to be saved?" he asks.

Paul and Silas smile at each other. "Just believe in the Lord Jesus and you will be saved, along with your family," they explain.

The jailer takes Paul and Silas to his home and gives them a meal. As the jailer takes care of their injuries, Paul and Silas tell him and his entire family about Jesus. They all believe in Jesus and are baptized. Then they celebrate!

To learn more about Paul and Silas in jail, read Acts 16:16-40.

A Rest Stop for Paul

The bus sets off on another long journey. "Are we still following Paul?" Munch asks. "He sure covered a lot of ground."

"And we're just seeing a few of the places he visited," Lana says. "He made a lot more stops."

"Looks like this stop will be in Corinth," Griffin says.

The smell of drying animal hide fills the air as Paul works. He is making a tent with his friends Aquila and Priscilla. Aquila and Priscilla are Jews who came to Corinth from Rome, Italy. They were forced to leave their home when the emperor decided to kick all the Jews out of Rome. Paul has been working with Aquila and Priscilla for a year and a half while they form a church in Corinth.

"This has been a wonderful time for me," Paul tells his friends. "When I came to Corinth, I wasn't expecting to find friends who would be my coworkers in tentmaking as well as church-making!"

Priscilla and Aquila laugh. "And when we had to leave our friends behind in Rome, we had no idea that God would give us so many wonderful new ones," Priscilla says.

"Including Jesus, the best Friend of all," Aquila adds. Priscilla nods.

After some time, Paul feels that his work in Corinth is finished and that God is calling him to move on. Priscilla and Aquila agree to go with him as far as Ephesus.

To learn more about Priscilla and Aquila, read Acts 18:1-3, 18-19.

CORINTH

- Corinth was one of the most important cities in Greece. It was located on the isthmus (land bridge) between the Ionian Sea and the Aegean Sea, on a major trading route.
- The Acrocorinth was a giant rock that rose almost 2,000 feet above sea level and overlooked the ancient city of Corinth. It was like a natural fortress, providing defense for the city.
- Corinth has hot, dry summers and cold, wet winters.
- The apostle Paul visited Corinth at least three times and wrote letters to the church there. Two of those letters are books in the Bible (1 and 2 Corinthians).

Fun Fact: According to Thucydides, a Greek historian and general, in 664 BC, Corinth became the first city to build warships.

A Dangerous Traffic Jam

Griffin consults the map. "If we're going to Ephesus, the quickest way to get there is by—" The bus splashes into the water. The raft inflates and the motor revs up. "—sea," finishes Griffin.

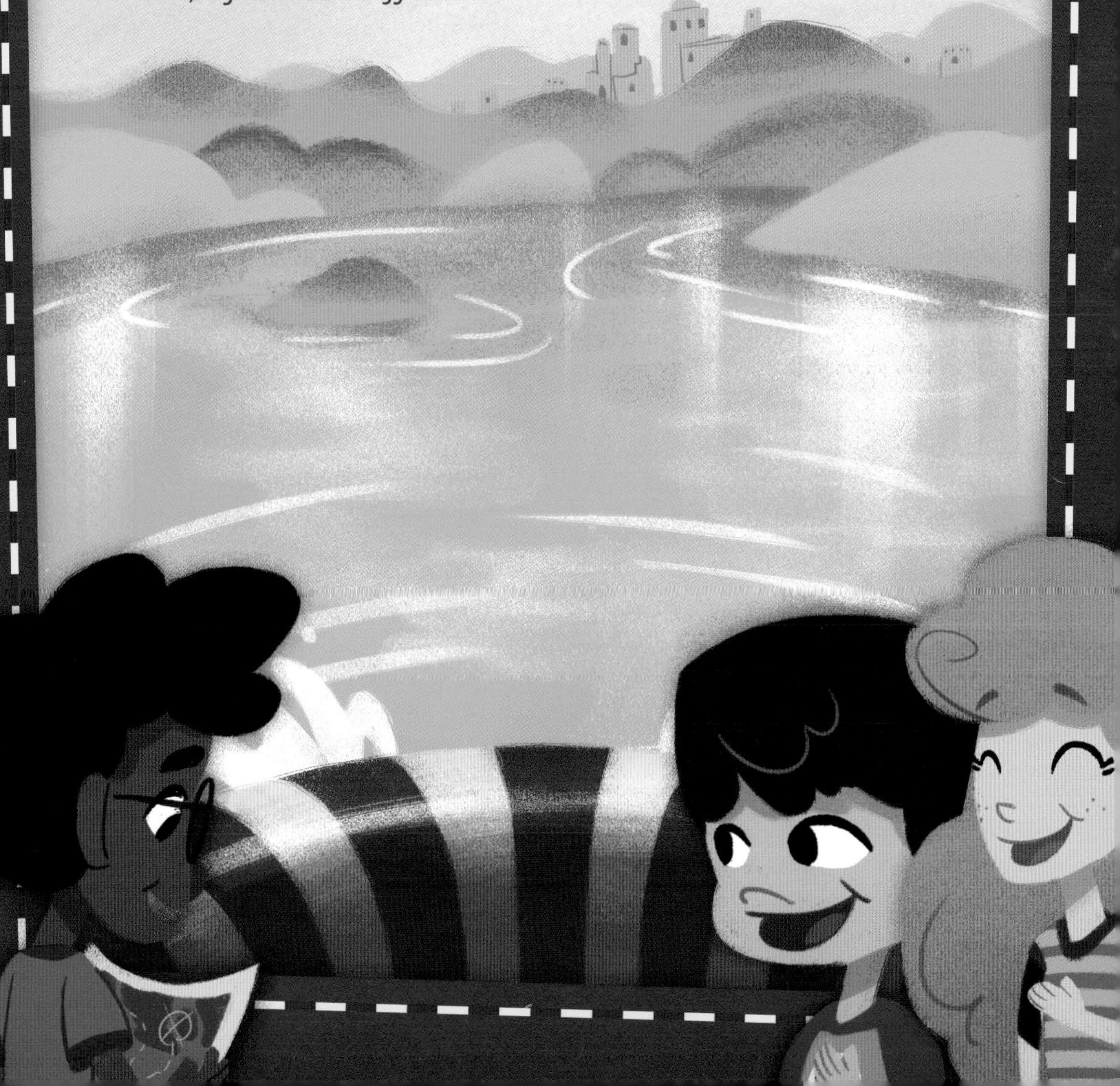

EPHESUS

- Ephesus was a city located along the western coast of modern Turkey. Because it was situated along the Aegean Sea and had one of the greatest seaports in the world, it was a center for trade and commerce.
- The climate in Ephesus was hot and dry in the summer and cold in the winter.
- Wealthy citizens of ancient Ephesus lived in terraced houses that were built into the sides of the mountain. Men and women had equal rights in Ephesus.
- The apostle Paul lived in Ephesus for three years.

Fun Fact: Some scholars believe that Mary, the mother of Jesus, lived in Ephesus during the last part of her life. It's said that the apostle John brought her to Ephesus and built her a home just outside the city. It is also believed that John wrote his Gospel in Ephesus.

Clink! Clink! Clink! The sound of hammers on metal fills the air in a busy Ephesian street. Demetrius the silversmith is putting the finishing touches on a statue of the Greek goddess Artemis. He stands back and admires his work. The sunlight reflects off the statue's face. Artemis is an important goddess for the Ephesians. There is even a temple in the city dedicated to her. And Demetrius is one of the best in Ephesus at making statues of her. He has many metalworkers and other craftsmen working for him. But Demetrius is not happy.

"All of this talk about Jesus and the 'one real God' is bad for business," he grumbles. "This Paul guy doesn't know when enough is enough." Demetrius looks around his shop. The silver statues and coins with Artemis's face on them are not selling as fast as usual. Some of his workers are even standing around with nothing to do! "Something needs to be done," Demetrius says.

Demetrius calls a meeting with the other craftsmen in the city. "This Paul character is telling everyone that our gods and goddesses are fake! He says there is only one true God. He's already caused our business to slow down a lot. Soon people will stop buying our statues of Artemis altogether." Everyone in the room looks worried. "We have to stop him!" Demetrius shouts. "It's not just that we're losing money, but the great goddess Artemis is losing her rightful glory! Soon Paul will bring down the temple of Artemis too!"

The craftsmen become furious. They begin to shout, "Great is Artemis of the Ephesians! Great is Artemis of the Ephesians!" They rush into the street, shouting and waving their fists in the air.

Before long, the entire city is filled with people shouting in the streets. Everyone starts rushing to the amphitheater, a huge building where they can all gather. A group of rioters finds Gaius and Aristarchus, who have been traveling with Paul, and drags them along to the amphitheater too.

Paul is very upset when he hears that his friends are in danger. "I should go to the amphitheater," he says.

But the other believers will not let Paul go. "That crowd is out of control!" they say. "It's much too dangerous." Messages start to arrive

from other friends of Paul, some of the area's most important people. "Paul, whatever you do, don't go to the amphitheater!" the messages read. "It's not worth risking your life."

Meanwhile, inside the amphitheater, the riot continues. Most of the people don't even know why they are there, but that doesn't stop them from making a lot of noise. A Jew named Alexander tries to get everyone to calm down, but that makes the Gentile Ephesians even angrier. "Great is Artemis of the Ephesians! Great is Artemis of the Ephesians!" they yell. They keep up their shouting for two whole hours.

THINK ABOUT IT!

The crowd . . . started shouting again and kept it up for about two hours: "Great is Artemis of the Ephesians! Great is Artemis of the Ephesians!"
Acts 19:34

The Temple of Artemis is one of the Seven Wonders of the Ancient World. It was a huge building made from marble, with many columns. Once a year, Ephesus put on a grand festival for the goddess Artemis. The festival included sports, plays, and musical concerts. Idols or statues of Artemis were an important part of worshiping the goddess. These statues are still sold in Ephesus today. The large statue of Artemis in the temple was believed to have fallen down from heaven.

SLOW!

Finally the mayor of Ephesus is able to get the people quiet enough to let him speak. "Citizens of Ephesus, you need to calm down," he says. "If Demetrius and his friends have a real problem, they have to settle it in court, like the law says. If this keeps up, the Romans will want to know why we are having a riot, and we won't have a good answer for them." The people listen to the mayor and go home. The riot is finally over.

To learn more about the riot in Ephesus, read Acts 19:23–20:1.

No Warm Welcome for Paul

The bus embarks from Ephesus and motors across the Mediterranean Sea. It rolls out of the water in Caesarea but keeps going over land. Finally, a very familiar city comes into view in the distance.

"Jerusalem again!" Munch exclaims.

Paul stands in the Temple with four other men. The four men have completed a special promise to God, and Paul is joining them in a purification ceremony. The leaders of the church in Jerusalem suggested that Paul do this to show that he still follows Jewish laws and doesn't preach against Moses or the Jewish Scriptures.

It is late on the last day of the ceremony, and Paul and his companions are almost ready to go home. Paul bows his head and thanks God for bringing him safely to Jerusalem.

Suddenly, rough hands grab Paul's arm. "Here he is!" an angry voice roars. "Men of Israel, help us deal with this troublemaker. He tells others not to abide by our laws. He even brings Gentiles into the Temple!"

"That's not true!" Paul protests. "I was with my Gentile friend Trophimus earlier today, but I didn't bring him in here!"

But nobody listens. An angry crowd forms. Someone grabs Paul's other arm, and someone else grabs his ankles. Paul is lifted off his feet and pulled this way and that. The mob drags him out of the Temple and starts to beat him. "Kill him! Kill him!" they yell. Paul tries to cover his face as he is hit with punches, slaps, and kicks.

"The Romans are coming! Here comes the commander with a troop of soldiers!" someone yells. The crowd stops beating Paul as the soldiers rush in among them. Several soldiers grab Paul and take him over to the commander.

"Is this the man who's causing all the commotion?" the commander asks, looking at Paul. "Chain him up." The soldiers put chains on Paul as the commander turns to the crowd. "Why are you beating this man?" he asks them. "Who is he? What has he done?"

Everyone tries to answer the commander at once. Some people yell one thing and some another. The commander shakes his head. "We're not going to get a sensible answer from this mob," he tells his soldiers. "Take the prisoner to the fortress. We'll see if we can straighten things out there."

As the soldiers take Paul away, the mob gets violent again. The soldiers hoist Paul onto their shoulders to protect him from the angry Jews. The crowd follows the soldiers to the fortress, shouting, "Kill him! Kill him!"

As Paul is about to be taken inside the fortress, he speaks to the commander. "Please let me talk to the people, sir," he requests. The commander agrees. Paul speaks to the Jews, telling them about how Jesus changed his life. "I am a Jew," Paul says to the people. "I follow the Jewish laws. Like you, I was eager to honor God. I thought it would make him happy if I attacked the followers of Jesus. But then Jesus himself met me on the road to Damascus and showed me that he is Lord." Paul tells the crowd about being blinded and then healed by Jesus. "When I got back to Jerusalem I had a vision in the Temple," Paul continues. "I saw Jesus again, and he told me to leave Jerusalem because you would not accept my testimony. The Lord Jesus sent me to tell the Gentiles about him."

BUILD YOUR FAITH!

Paul traveled around the world and spoke openly about his faith as a Christian, even though people hurt him because of it. Do you speak with others about your faith without being afraid of how they might respond? When is the last time you told someone about Jesus?

When Paul says the word *Gentiles*, the crowd goes wild with fury. "Kill him!" they shout even louder. They throw their coats on the ground and fling handfuls of dust into the air.

The commander brings Paul inside the fortress. The next day, the commander calls a meeting of the Jewish high council and brings Paul before them. "Maybe now we can figure out what is going on here," he says. Paul tries to speak to the council, but things soon get ugly again. The commander takes Paul back into the fortress to keep him from being killed. That night, Paul sees the Lord in a dream. "Be encouraged, Paul," the Lord says. "You have told people about me in Jerusalem, and you will do the same in Rome."

The next morning, Paul's nephew comes to see him. "I heard about a plot to kill you," he warns his uncle. "Some Jews took an oath to not eat or drink anything until you are dead!"

When the commander hears about the plot, he sends Paul to Caesarea with some of his soldiers. "Governor Felix can decide what to do with you," he says.

But Governor Felix can't make up his mind about Paul. He leaves him in jail until a new governor, Festus, comes to town. The Jews try to persuade Festus to send Paul back to Jerusalem. They plan to kill Paul along the way. But Paul tells Festus, "I am a Roman citizen. It's my right to have the emperor, Caesar, decide my case. Send me to Rome!"

"All right," Festus agrees. "I will send you to Caesar. To Rome you will go!"

To learn more about Paul's arrest and time in prison, read Acts 21:18–26:32.

BUILD YOUR FAITH!

When Paul traveled to Corinth, God provided him with friends. Paul met people who shared his faith and passion for spreading the Good News about Jesus. Who do you know who gets excited about the same things you do or who has similar dreams for the future? Thank God for your friends right now!

A Difficult Journey

"This is the last journey of Paul recorded in the Bible," Lana tells her friends. "It's a long trip to Rome."

"A long trip?" Munch says. "It can't be as long as the trip we've been on."

"Yeah," Lana agrees. "But you have to admit, this trip has been pretty amazing."

"Hate to break it to you guys," Griffin says, "but I don't think we are going all the way to Rome yet. I remember this story—it's not smooth sailing."

Waves as big as buildings crash against the sides and over the deck of a wooden ship. A terrible wind howls and raindrops come down so fast that they sting the skin of the sailors and passengers who cling desperately to whatever they can find, trying not to be swept overboard.

"Hang on, Paul!" a Roman officer named Julius yells as Paul's hands slip from the railing. Julius grabs Paul and helps him get a better grip.

"Thank you, Julius," Paul gasps. Julius has been kind to Paul during this long journey. He's even let him visit his friends whenever they make a stop on land.

"Are Luke and Aristarchus all right?" Paul asks Julius.

The Roman nods. "They're over there," he yells over the wind, pointing across the deck. Paul's two friends are clinging to ropes, swinging back and forth as the ship is tossed up and down on the waves.

CRETE

- Crete is a large island in the Mediterranean Sea, just south of Greece. It has many mountains, forests, and natural harbors.
- The island had many people and hundreds of cities. It has mild winters and warm, dry summers.
- People who lived on the island of Crete are often called Minoans. The Minoans were excellent sailors. They were also very good with bows and arrows.
- The Minoans produced timber, wine, oil, cloth, and purple dye and sold them to other nations.

Fun Fact: People from Crete were present at Pentecost (see Acts 2:11).

"All the cargo has been thrown overboard. The sailors have even dumped some of the ship's equipment," Julius says. "I don't know how much longer we can hang on."

Paul struggles to stand, clinging to the rail. "Listen up, everyone!" he roars. The exhausted sailors and passengers look at him. "You should have paid attention to me back in Crete," Paul says. "I told you this was going to happen. But cheer up! One of God's angels came to me last night and told me that we will lose the ship, but we will all survive!"

The storm rages on for days. Finally, around midnight on the 14th day of the storm, the sailors discover that the water is getting shallower and shallower. "If this keeps up, we'll be washed up on the rocks!" they say. "Pray for daylight!"

find something to hang on to!" Everyone jumps into the water. Every sailor, soldier, passenger, and prisoner makes it to the shore, soaked and shivering—but alive, just as the angel promised.

Paul lies on the sandy beach, happy to feel solid ground under him again. He looks up when he hears footsteps, and he sees a smiling man standing next to him. "Welcome to the island of Malta," the man says, helping Paul stand up. "You have a strange way of traveling."

The men, women, and children of Malta run back and forth, bringing the survivors over to a huge fire they have built. "Come and warm up," they say. They treat everyone kindly, soldiers and prisoners alike.

MALTA

- Malta is a tiny island in the middle of the Mediterranean Sea, just south of Sicily.
- Over the years, many different nations influenced Malta, making the culture very diverse.
- The earliest inhabitants of Malta were most likely Sicilians. They grew grains and raised livestock on the island.

Fun Fact: Paul's ship wrecked on the northern coast of the island, in what is now called St. Paul's Bay.

Once Paul has gotten warm, he decides to help out. "I'll get some more wood so we can keep this fire going," he says. Soon he has an armful of sticks. As he starts to put them on the fire, a snake lunges out of the bundle and bites Paul's hand, hanging on to it by the fangs.

The islanders gasp in horror. "That man must be a vicious murderer," they whisper to each other. "He survived the shipwreck, but justice is punishing him with a snakebite. That snake is extremely poisonous. Soon he will start to swell up, and then he'll drop dead."

But Paul shakes the snake off into the fire and keeps gathering firewood. Everyone watches Paul for hours, waiting for something to happen. But nothing does. The people are amazed. "He must be a god," they say to each other.

Publius, the chief official of the island, lives nearby. He comes to welcome the survivors of the shipwreck. "Don't worry about anything," he says. "We will take care of you until you are able to continue your journey." Publius hosts the survivors in his home for three days. While they are there, Paul learns that Publius's father is very sick. Paul goes to see him and prays for him. Then Paul places his hands on Publius's father and heals him. "How can I ever thank you?" Publius exclaims.

When the islanders hear about the healing, they bring their sick family members to Paul. With God's help, he heals every one of them.

After three months, Paul, the Roman soldiers, and the other prisoners board another ship that spent the winter in Malta. Finally, Paul is once again on his way to Rome.

ROME

- Rome was founded in 753 BC. It was the capital of the ancient Roman Empire and today is the capital of Italy.
- Rome is known for its systems of aqueducts, structures that were built to carry water around the city.
- People in ancient Rome lived in apartments and ate cereal, grains, bread, milk, cheese, meats, fish, and eggs.
- Romans bathed in public bathhouses, which often included a pool, heat room, library, and lecture hall. Men and women had separate bathhouses.
- Clothing in Rome was used to designate one's social status.
- The language spoken in Rome was Latin. Many of today's languages, such as Spanish, Portuguese, French, Italian, and Romanian, came from Latin.

Fun Fact: The Colosseum is the largest amphitheater (a round building with levels of seats rising around an open space) in the world. About 50,000 people could fit in it. Ancient Romans used to watch gladiator fights and other shows there.

"Spinning sprockets!" Munch says. "I thought for sure that Paul was a goner when that snake bit him."

"God has bigger plans for Paul," Lana says.

"I've always wanted to go to Rome!" Griffin waves the map excitedly.

Paul stares at the Roman buildings outside his window. He smiles at the Roman citizens as they pass by. *I finally made it!* he says to himself. Paul has his own house in Rome, but a soldier stands outside the door. Paul is under house arrest. But he is allowed to have as many visitors as he wants. For the next two years, Paul welcomes both Jews and Gentiles, telling everyone who comes to see him about the Lord Jesus and his Kingdom.

To learn more about Paul's journey to Rome, read Acts 27–28.

The End of the Road?

"Bye, Paul!" Lana waves out the back window as the bus leaves Rome. Griffin picks up the Bible from Lana's seat.

"Is that it for Paul?" he asks. "What happens to him next?"

"He is released and does some more traveling, but a few years later, he is imprisoned again . . . and executed," Lana says.

"Man," Griffin says. "So many of Jesus' disciples were killed for following him."

"Yeah," Lana replies. "Church tradition says that the only one of the 12 apostles who wasn't killed for his faith was John, although he was exiled on an island called—"

"Patmos?" asks Munch, looking out the window.

"Yes," Lana says, surprised. "How did you know?"

Munch points. While the friends have been talking, the bus has arrived on the shore of a small island. A sign stuck into the pebbly beach reads, "Patmos."

John has been sent to the island of Patmos because the Jews and the Romans did not like him preaching about Jesus and leading the church. The Jews have convinced the Roman rulers that Jesus' followers are dangerous, and Christians are being put in prison and sometimes even killed for their beliefs. John is a prisoner in the Roman fortress on the island.

One Sunday, John is worshiping God when he hears a trumpet blast and a loud voice right behind him! John jumps, startled. "Write down everything you're about to see," the voice says.

PATMOS

- The island of Patmos is located in the Aegean Sea near Greece. It is very rocky and has very few trees.
- Patmos is very small, only about seven miles long and six miles wide.
- The Romans sent criminals to Patmos as punishment. Prisoners probably had to work in mines there.

Fun Fact: Books as we know them did not exist during Bible times. John wrote the book of Revelation on a scroll. The form of book that we know today, with pages between two covers, is called a *codex*.

John turns around and sees seven lamps made of gold. Standing in the middle of the lamps is a man whose face shines like the sun and whose eyes blaze like fire. His hair is bright white, and his voice sounds like the crashing of thousands of waves in the ocean. He has seven stars in his hand and a sharp sword coming out of his mouth!

John falls down on his face in front of the man, completely terrified. The man lays his right hand on John and says, "Don't be afraid! I am the First and the Last, the one who died but is now alive forever! Write down what I tell you and what I show you."

John realizes that it is Jesus who is talking to him! He faithfully writes down everything as Jesus instructs him.

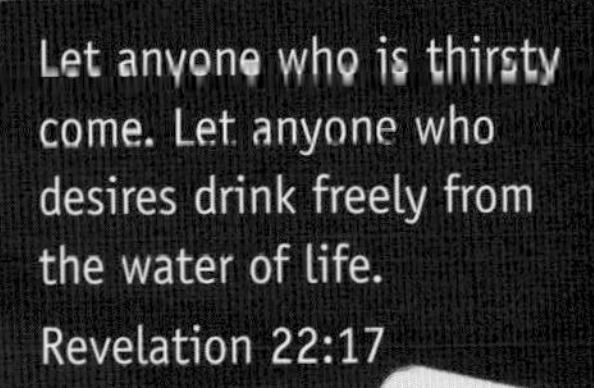

Let anyone who is thirsty come. Let anyone who desires drink freely from the water of life.

Revelation 22:17

PARK HERE!

READ AND MEMORIZE THIS VERSE.

John writes Jesus' special messages to seven churches. He records his glorious vision of God on his throne, describing heaven as best as he can. He writes down what God shows him about the future and the end of the world. He writes of the beautiful things that God's people will enjoy in the new heaven and the new earth—a city made of gold and precious jewels, a wonderful tree with healing leaves, and a river that flows with the water of life.

Finally, Jesus tells John, "I am the Alpha and the Omega, the First and the Last, the Beginning and the End. Let anyone who is thirsty come and drink from the water of life. I am coming soon!"

John finally finishes writing everything down. "Yes! Come, Lord Jesus!" he says. He can't wait for what God has shown him to come true.

To learn more about John's incredible vision, read the book of Revelation.

Conclusion

"Oh!" Lana squeals. "I can't wait for Jesus to come again! It will be so—" Suddenly, the bus starts spinning. Lana grabs onto the seat in front of her, trying not to fall.

"What's happening?" Munch shouts. "Where are we going now?"

The bus finally comes to a stop. Griffin looks outside. "I think we went home," he says. "There's the church and Pastor Rick's window."

Lana starts to let go of the seat but quickly grabs back on as the bus shakes violently. The leather seat tears beneath her fingers. Stunned, she looks around. All of the seats have changed back into the shabby ones she remembers from the beginning of their adventure.

The bus shakes again. Munch braces himself against the seat. "Spinning sprockets!" he says, tracing one of the huge cracks that have spread down the windows. He winces as a small sliver of glass lodges in his fingertip. Munch watches in one of the rearview mirrors as the minibus's sparkling red paint fades and becomes spotted with rust.

The kids cover their ears at the sound of loud popping. The bus sinks a bit as the tires flatten. Then everything is quiet for a moment. Lana, Munch, and Griffin stare at each other, not sure what to do next.

Finally, a voice breaks the silence. "You kids better come inside," Pastor Rick calls through his office window. "Lunch period is nearly over."

Griffin glances at his watch. "In 58 seconds the bell is going to ring. We've only been gone 13 minutes," he says. No one speaks or moves for a few seconds.

"Griffin, do you remember what Mrs. Morgan said about knowing God?" Lana whispers.

"Yeah," Griffin replies. "The best way to get to know God is to read his Word."

"Well, I feel like I know God a lot better now," Lana says.

"Me, too," Griffin says.

"Me three," Munch chimes in.

"Let's get off this bus," Lana says. "I have the most amazing images racing through my mind. I want to go inside and draw everything that we saw."

"That's a great idea!" Griffin says. "Need some help drawing the maps?"

The door of the minibus swings wide open. Munch pushes past the other two kids and runs off the bus, almost knocking Lana over.

"What's the rush?" Lana shouts.

"Are you kidding?" Munch hollers back. "We just traveled through time! We're time travelers! No, wait—we're *Story* Travelers! My head is spinning with new inventions." He disappears inside Pastor Rick's office.

"Story Travelers," Griffin repeats. "I like the sound of that." He stands up. "Come on, Lana," he says. "Let's go inside and draw our pictures. Then we can tell all the other kids about our adventures on the minibus."

Lana laughs, and they enter the church building, waving to Pastor Rick as they walk by. "No one will believe us," she says.

Pastor Rick smiles. Once the kids are out of sight, he looks out his office window. "At least one person will," he says, gazing at the rusted minibus on the church lawn.